Love Your Goldfish
and Fancy Coldwater Fish

Golden Orfe

Green Tench

Love Your Goldfish
and Fancy Coldwater Fish

Don Harper

W. Foulsham & Co. Ltd.

London ● New York ● Toronto ● Cape Town ● Sydney

W. Foulsham & Company Limited
Yeovil Road, Slough, Berkshire, SL1 4JH

ISBN 0-572-01239-X

Printed in Spain by Cayfosa, Barcelona.
Dep. Leg. B-27227-1986

Contents

1 **Keeping Goldfish**

The goldfish (*Carassius auratus*) was first kept solely as an ornamental fish in China, where it was being bred by AD 800. These highly coloured fish are thought to have been derived from the dull Wild Goldfish of that period, which were maintained as a source of food. From China, ornamental goldfish were introduced to Japan by AD 1500 and first reached Europe during the seventeenth century. They were initially kept in ponds, and bred freely under such conditions. The English statesman Horace Walpole sent goldfish from his own ponds to Italy and Russia shortly afterwards, and others were dispatched to the Netherlands, where they soon bred.

The development of the so-called 'fancy' varieties of the goldfish, all derived from the original colour mutant, began in China, and today a wide range of such fish are available. These generally require more careful management than the Common Goldfish, and not all forms can be kept satisfactorily in ponds.

The goldfish is a member of the Cyprinidae, sometimes referred to as the Carp family. In common with other members of this group, they can live to ten years or more if kept properly. Unfortunately, this was not always the case in the past, but now, with the development of special foods and treatments for sick fish, it is very easy to keep coldwater fish healthy. The size of a goldfish does not give an accurate indication of its age, however, since generally those kept in relatively small surroundings do not grow as big as individuals living in large ponds. There are records of pond fish growing to 60 cm (2 ft) in length.

Scale Structure

The scales protect the fish's body, and have a tightly overlapping structure. They do not increase in number as the fish grows, but simply expand in size. Since the number of scales is relatively constant, this figure is used to assist with the classification of fish. There are, for example, between 25 and 30 scales running along the lateral line in the case of the goldfish, whereas the Common Carp (*Cyprinus carpio*) has 34 to 40 in this region.

The appearance of goldfish is actually influenced by light being reflected back through the scales, via cells known as iridocytes. In the normal situation when this happens, the goldfish have a relatively shiny appearance, and are therefore referred to as being 'metallic'.

By way of contrast, when the reflective tissue below the scales is reduced, a mother-of-pearl type effect is created. Such fish are now described as 'nacreous', although formerly the term 'calico' was used. It is incorrect to refer to nacreous fish as 'scaleless', since the scales themselves are unaffected. Nacreous goldfish usually have a mottled appearance.

In the third category, where the iridocytes are completely absent, the goldfish will be a dull pinkish colour, and are known as 'matt'.

They have no lustre whatsoever, and are not as popular as the other types.

Certain varieties of goldfish can be obtained in all these various forms, whereas others, by definition, as explained later, have to be of one particular type.

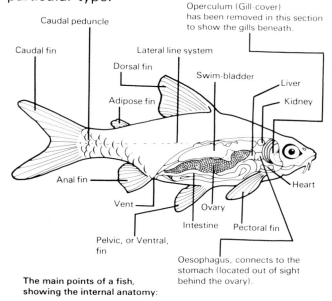

The main points of a fish, showing the internal anatomy:

- Caudal peduncle
- Caudal fin
- Lateral line system
- Dorsal fin
- Adipose fin
- Anal fin
- Vent
- Pelvic, or Ventral, fin
- Intestine
- Ovary
- Pectoral fin
- Swim-bladder
- Liver
- Kidney
- Heart
- Operculum (Gill-cover) has been removed in this section to show the gills beneath.
- Oesophagus, connects to the stomach (located out of sight behind the ovary).

Colour

The actual colour of goldfish results primarily from three colour pigments, which are yellow, black and reddish-orange. These are located at various depths within the body tissue, and since they can therefore overlap, additional colours can be produced. When all pigments are absent, however, in the case of the metallic group for example, the fish are silver, as a direct result of the unpigmented tissue beneath the scales.

Purchasing Goldfish

Goldfish are still imported to Europe from the Far East, with large consignments being sent by air, especially during late spring and early summer. There are also very large goldfish breeding establishments in the United States, supplying millions of fish to the pet trade each year. On dealers' premises, however, with a large throughput of fish, the opportunity for disease to spread multiplies manifold, even before the goldfish have reached their final point of sale.

Several rules must therefore be followed to ensure, as far as possible, that only healthy fish are selected in the first instance. When looking at goldfish before buying, it is worth noting the surroundings where they are being kept. There should be no dead or sickly individuals in the same pond or tank, and ideally the vendor should be using a separate net when catching from each group, to prevent the spread of disease.

Healthy fish appear active, and swim without difficulty. Their fins should be in good condition, with no ragged or frayed edges. The body must appear clean, and be free from any trace of fungus (which may create a halo effect), white spots or ulcers. The eyes should be clear and not swollen, although they will be distorted in the case of telescope-eyed varieties. There must also be no apparent swelling of the belly, which may otherwise indicate of dropsy. If in any doubt about a fish, it is always better not to buy it. Apart from the risk of introducing disease to established stock, sickly fish will be a source of considerable work, and may well be beyond saving.

While goldfish are commercially imported in large numbers, a significant proportion are also bred by amateurs. Stock purchased direct from a local breeder often proves the best investment, although it may be slightly more expensive.

Obviously it is much better to see the fish personally, but on occasions, when seeking a particular variety for example, this may not be possible. The breeder concerned might be prepared however to dispatch the fish, usually at the buyer's risk, by train. When seeking goldfish for exhibition purposes, it is often difficult with young stock to assess their later appearance and show potential. Their characteristic features may take several years to develop, as in the case of the Lionhead and related varieties. Gaining some experience with the Common Goldfish is to be recommended though, before progressing to these more difficult and expensive forms.

2 Varieties

The number of fancy varieties which have been bred from the Common Goldfish is almost incalculable. One Chinese author has estimated that at least 126 distinct recognised forms are known, but in reality, with various metallic, nacreous and matt forms of these fish, as well as differences in eye structure, the total probably exceeds this figure.

Some breeds are virtually unknown outside the particular area of the Far East where they originated. One example of this type is the Outfolded Operculum which remains confined largely to northern China. In this case, there is a modification of the gill cover (operculum), which may leave the gills themselves exposed. It has acquired a reputation for being a delicate fish.

An indication of the popularity of particular breeds in Britain can be obtained from the standards laid down by the Goldfish Society of Great Britain. Eight basic and five popular varieties are recognised by this organisation for show purposes. The varieties in the following section here are listed in alphabetical order, for ease of reference, with particular emphasis being given to the more common varieties.

Bubble-eye

Alternative name: Water Bubble-eye.
Suitability: Aquarium.
The Bubble-eye is a Chinese breed, especially popular in the province of Kwangtung. Their name is derived from swellings which resemble bubbles, extending from the lower border of each eye socket. These sacs are filled with a gelatinous-type substance, which can be seen to reverberate as the fish moves through the water. Bubble-eyes should only be kept in tanks free from sharp projections, because their eye sacs are easily punctured.

The body shape of the Bubble-eye closely corresponds to that of the Celestial, although the eyes themselves are positioned normally, but relatively closely to the top of the head. Bubble-eyes have been bred in a range of colours, in both metallic and nacreous forms.

Celestial

Alternative names: Sky-gazer (Ch'aot'ienyen); Heavenward Dragon.
Suitability: Aquarium.
The Celestial takes its name from the skyward positioning of its eyes, which also protrude outwards from the body. Perhaps not surprisingly, as a result of this deviation, these goldfish can encounter difficulties in catching livefood, and are best kept together in groups, rather than being mixed with other varieties. Celestials are often rather pinkish in colour, although an extremely rare black form has been recorded from China.

Another characteristic of the Celestial is the

absence of a dorsal fin, which has led the Chinese to include the term 'dragon' in its alternative name. This description is applied to all goldfish lacking a dorsal fin.

Comet

Suitability: Pond or aquarium.
This breed was initially developed in America, by Hugo Mullert of Philadelphia in the early nineteenth century. Its distinctive tail is almost as long as its body, with the caudal fin being very deeply-forked. The other fins also tend to taper to a point, rather than being rounded in shape.

The colour of the Comet ranges from a deep reddish-orange to yellow, with examples of this latter colour also being described as 'Canary Fish'. There is a blue variety known, but this is presently rare. The so-called Sarasa Comets, which are red and white, have become more popular during recent years and are equally easy to cater for, proving quite hardy.

Comets are quite active fish by nature, and thus probably more suited to life in a pond rather than an aquarium. Breeding results are often better when Comets are housed in spacious surroundings. If kept indoors, then a rectangular tank of good length is essential.

Common Goldfish

Suitability: Aquarium or pond.
This is the original mutant form, derived from Wild Goldfish, which has in turn become the ancestor of all the other varieties seen today.

Comet

Common Goldfish

The Common Goldfish can grow to a size of 45 cm (18 ins) or so under exceptional conditions, and, in spite of its name, has been bred in a range of colours, from white to yellow and deep reddish-orange. These so-called 'self' colours, apart from white, are more popular than the variegated forms such as red or yellow and silver combinations. Black markings are sometimes seen, but these prove transitory and are not a sign of illness.

The ideal shape of the Common Goldfish should convey a balanced impression, with the body being stocky, and curving equally top and bottom. The fins must be in proportion to the body, while the head itself needs to be short and broad. Spawning occurs more readily under pond conditions, although under these circumstances, it then is difficult to assess the quality of the young fish, and they can fall prey to other occupants of the pond.

Fantail

Suitability: Pond or aquarium.
Fantails have a relatively oval body shape, compared to the Common Goldfish, and are thought to be descended from the Ryukin. They differ, however, by lacking the slight hump present in the neck region of the Ryukin, and being less broad overall. The characteristic caudal fins are paired, being linked together at their base. The tail must be erect, showing no signs of drooping. The anal fins are also divided.

The Fantail is not a large variety, reaching a maximum size of 10 cm (4 ins) or so, but unlike other fancy goldfish, these fish are relatively hardy and may be overwintered successfully

Common Goldfish

Red Fantail

under pond conditions, if provided with an adequate depth of water. They will also breed readily in aquaria, although the production of good exhibition specimens is not easy. A telescope-eyed form of the Fantail has also been established.

Lionhead

Alternative names: Hooded Goldfish; Buffalo-head; Tomato-head; Ranchu.
Suitability: Aquarium.
These goldfish are characterised by their peculiarly modified heads, which are covered in a warty-like excrescence resembling raspberries. This feature in turn was then imparted to the Oranda. The body shape of the Lionhead resembles that of the Veiltail, although its finnage corresponds more closely to Fantails. A dorsal fin is absent.

Moor

Alternative name: Black Moor.
Suitability: Aquarium.
The Moor is characterised by its distinctive coloration, which should be jet black, although this is hard to achieve and even more difficult to retain. Fish tend to become paler as they age, and so the Moor's coloration takes on a bronzy hue, rather than remaining black. Another feature of this variety is its protuberant eyes. Their telescope eyes are actually located in a normal position, although in rare instances, they may be directed either forwards or downwards. In actual appearance, the Moor corresponds to the Veiltail.

Lionhead

Moor

Oranda

Alternative names: Dutch Lionhead (Japanese); Goose-head; Frog-head.
Suitability: Aquarium
This variety resembles the Veiltail, although it also possesses the warty-like growth on the head seen in the Lionhead. Orandas were evolved in Japan by crossing the two varieties mentioned previously, from 1840 onwards. They are most commonly a combination of red and white, but black individuals, and odd examples with a red body and yellow belly are also known. A brownish form, known as the Chocolate is presently being bred in larger numbers, and being seen more commonly as a result. These relatively dull fish show to best effect under a light in an aquarium. The Red Oranda is basically whitish, with a red cap on its head, equivalent to that of the Lionhead. Blue Orandas are a combination of blue and white in colour, and have recently been developed on a large scale in the United States. Remember that Orandas are not suitable to be kept in ponds throughout the year, and will have to be brought inside for the winter, although they may well be offered as pond fish. They are not fast swimmers, and are likely to be at a disadvantage when competing alongside other fish for food.

Pearlscale

Suitability: Aquarium.
Fish of this type are instantly recognisable by their scales, which have raised centres and dark perimeters. Their pearl-like appearance results from the reflection of light off the scales

Lionhead

Pearlscale

themselves. This breed is thought to have originated in China, where it is still popular, especially in the province of Kwangtung. It was probably first introduced to western aquarists from Japan. A goldfish corresponding to the Pearlscale was received in America about 1897, where it became known initially as the Barnacle. The Pearlscale has a very fat body coupled with a relatively straight back and an apparently swollen belly. It is normally silver in colour coupled with distinct reddish areas.

Pompon

Alternative name: Velvet Ball.
Suitability: Aquarium.
The Pompon at first sight may appear similar to a hooded Lionhead, but can be immediately distinguished because its swellings, known as narial bouquets, are developed from the nostrils. These two outgrowths must be balanced in size, although their size is quite variable, ranging from little bigger than a fish's eye to almost a third of the head in area, which may be sucked into the mouth repeatedly.

The origins of the Pompon have been lost, but the variety was known in Japan during the last century. It was introduced to both Britain and France by about 1936, but remains one of the rare breeds. Various forms have been evolved, with one group lacking a dorsal fin. Occasional white or orange examples have been reported, but mixed coloration is most common.

Bubble-Eye

Bristol Shubunkin

Shubunkin

Alternative names: Speckled Goldfish; Harlequin Goldfish; Coronation Fish.
Suitability: Pond or aquarium.
The Shubunkin is a form of the Common Goldfish, which differs simply in its scale structure. Two distinct types of Shubunkin are recognised. The London Shubunkin is merely the traditional nacreous counterpart of the Common Goldfish, whereas the Bristol Shubunkin is similar, but has a modified fin structure, with the caudal fin being both enlarged and rounded. These fish grow smaller than the London variety, which can reach 25 cm (10 ins) in size. Shubunkins are generally reliable breeders and ideal for a pond, where they can be kept throughout the year. They are active by nature, and require a large aquarium if they are to be kept indoors.

Toadhead

Suitability: Aquarium.
These goldfish closely resemble Celestials, but can be distinguished by the presence of swellings below the eyes. These are said to create the appearance resembling that of a toad, hence the name.

Veiltail

Alternative names: Fringetail; Ribbontail.
Suitability: Aquarium.
The Veiltail was developed in America, around Philadelphia, during the last century. Its name is derived from its modified caudal fin, which is divided and enlarged, to form a paired, flowing tail with a square edge. The other fins

Shubunkin

Veiltail

are also enlarged, with the dorsal being especially prominent. They are, however, easily damaged and so these goldfish should be kept together in aquaria where there are no sharp projections on rockwork. The body of the Veiltail is spherical, and both normal and telescope-eyed forms are recognised. When crossed with the Common Goldfish, Veiltails give rise to a variety known as the Watonai. Single-tailed Veiltails with a single anal fin, normally discarded by serious breeders, are sometimes referred to as 'Nymphs'.

Other Goldfish Varieties

There are other varieties of eastern origin which remain rare elsewhere in the world. The Brocade or *Kinransi*, for example originated in Japan, being established by Akiyama Kichigoro about 1905. It resembles the Common Goldfish in shape, although the dorsal fin is absent, while its body coloration is mixed. Perhaps one of the most unusual goldfish is the so-called Blue Fish, or *Lan-yii* in Chinese. It was seen in America by the 1880s, while some completely blue goldfish were also bred in Britain during the 1930s, although this particular strain appears to have been lost. The Chinese Blue Fish were a dark blue in colour, apparently resembling the Moor in other respects. The challenge of recreating these fish and breeding new forms still fascinates breeders today.

Blue Shubunkin

Golden Orfe

3 **Housing**

The choice of accommodation for goldfish will be determined by several factors, such as the varieties to be kept, and personal circumstances. As emphasised in the previous chapter, the more fancy forms of the goldfish are not hardy, and therefore have to be kept indoors in temperate climates. An aquarium, however, provides the ideal means of appreciating the fin or body embellishments of such fish at close quarters. In contrast, goldfish kept in a pond will add colour and movement to what may otherwise be an attractive yet static scene for much of the year.

Aquaria

Glass goldfish bowls have now thankfully almost completely vanished. Apart from allowing little swimming space, the globular shape of these bowls spelt disaster for many of their occupants. It is always important when choosing any tank to take into account the surface area at the air-water interface. This is where oxygen enters the water, and is then extracted by the flow of water over the fish's gills. In goldfish bowls which were filled up to the top with water, the surface area was too small to allow a satisfactory oxygen content in the water.

A rectangular tank is always preferable, offering a combination of better swimming space and oxygenation of the water. Matching components, such as filters and hoods, are more easily obtainable for this design of aquarium. The cheapest and most popular glass tanks today are bonded together very effectively with a special silicone rubber sealant, and no longer require a heavy metal framework and putty to hold the glass in place. In addition, this sealer does not dry out like putty, so such tanks should not spring leaks unexpectedly, as is especially likely to occur with puttied tanks which have been empty for a period of time. Frameless tanks must, however, always stand on a base of polystyrene.

Plastic tanks, made in one unit, are also now widely available, especially smaller sizes. They are lighter than glass aquaria of the same size, but tend to scratch very easily. The plastic may also become discoloured over a period of time which spoils the enjoyment of watching the fish in the aquarium. Plastic aquaria are very useful, however, as spare tanks, for isolation or breeding purposes.

The size of tank chosen depends partly on the variety, as well as the number of goldfish which are being kept together. Moors, for example, do not grow much larger than 12.5 cm (5 ins) or so, whereas London Shubunkins can reach double this size. Adequate allowance must be made for the subsequent growth of the fish, and it pays to select a relatively large tank in the first place.

Having bought a tank, it must be washed out thoroughly before use in order to remove any dirt or minute slivers of glass which may otherwise harm the fish. Disinfectants and detergents used in the home are generally dangerous for use with fish, since even minute amounts remaining after a thorough rinsing can prove toxic. A solution of salt water, made up on the basis of 28 g (1 oz) of salt to 4.5 litres (1 gallon) of water is a quite effective alternative for general aquarium usage, with the tank or equipment being washed off afterwards.

Other Equipment

The use of an aquarium filter will help to keep the aquarium clean, avoiding the need to empty the tank regularly. There are various types of filter available, with the undergravel form being probably the simplest. This filter is designed to fit into the bottom of the tank,

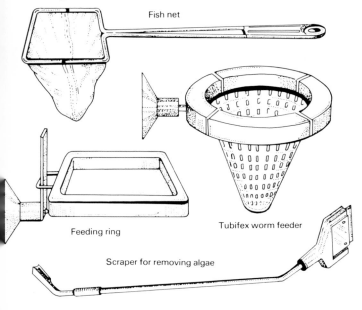

Fish net

Feeding ring

Tubifex worm feeder

Scraper for removing algae

Useful tank equipment

covering the whole length, and must be connected to an air pump. Aquarium gravel, to a minimum depth of 7.5 cm (3 ins) needs to be placed on top of the filter. Once the tank is set up, beneficial aerobic bacteria will develop in the gravel. Then, as debris from the fish is drawn down through the gravel by the action of the pump, these bacteria break the waste products down to safe, beneficial compounds such as nitrate, which can then be used by the plants for their growth.

It is important to keep the air pump running round the clock, to maintain the effectiveness of the system. The cost of running a pump is very low, although it will pay to purchase a good quality pump as cheap pumps tend to be noisier, although noise can be reduced by standing the pump on a felt pad. Pumps must never be covered, as they will rapidly become a fire hazard.

An air pump is also necessary to operate a box-type filter, which may fit either inside or outside the aquarium. The water from the tank is pumped up and filtered through the box where the debris remains. Such filters must contain two layers of special filter wool, with charcoal in between. Gravel is often added as well, to weigh down the contents of the filter. The charcoal helps to remove toxic waste compounds in solution, while the wool acts as a mesh to filter out solid particles. Box filters need to be cleaned out every three weeks or so, when their components must be changed, to remain effective.

A hood, or some other form of cover, will be necessary for the aquarium. It will help to prevent excessive evaporation and stop the water becoming contaminated with dust. Hoods are made in a range of sizes to suit particular tanks and usually include space for a light.

Lighting above the aquarium is beneficial, primarily to encourage plant growth, as well as showing the fish to good effect. Some fluorescent tubes are specifically for use with plants, since they cover the natural light spectrum, and so will stimulate their growth.

A dealer will be able to advise on the required wattage, depending on the size of the tank. Excessive lighting will, however, lead to build-up of algae in the aquarium, and it may be necessary to experiment to find the optimum amount of light to give good plant growth while ensuring algae are kept in check. As a guide, a 20 watt fluorescent tube is sufficient for a 60 cm (24 inch) aquarium, being left on for eight hours or so each day.

Siting

The positioning of the aquarium in the room is important, to avoid later problems. It must be located away from direct sunlight, because otherwise excessive algal growth is likely and the water temperature may rise too high for the fish's comfort. As the temperature of water rises, so its oxygen content falls. The tank will also need to be sited relatively close to an electrical point, to avoid trailing wires, and at a convenient height for maintenance purposes. It is also important to choose an area in the room where the fish can be fully appreciated.

A permanent site will be necessary, because especially with a large aquarium, once full, the weight of water will make it impossible to shift without emptying it. A firm level surface, able to support the weight of the tank, will be essential, and so an aquarium stand may be required. A dechlorinator will need to be added to the water so that it is safe for the fish.

Types of Ponds

Ponds come in all shapes and sizes. There are now two main options to consider when constructing a pond in the average garden: pool liners, which come in the form of thick heavy duty sheeting, and moulded fibreglass pools. Irrespective of the type of pond, however, it is vital to ensure that the width of the excavation exceeds its depth. In areas where the water is likely to freeze in winter, the depth should be about 90 cm (3 ft) to ensure adequate protection for the fish.

Fibreglass Ponds

Fibreglass ponds are simply placed in a pre-dug hole, and then packed around with soil to keep them firm. Unfortunately the majority are not deep enough to allow the goldfish to overwinter successfully. They must therefore be caught up in the autumn and transferred to an aquarium.

Filters and Pumps

Filters are not normally required for goldfish ponds, but if waterfalls or fountains are desired, then an electrical pump will be necessary. There are two types available, and it is again preferable to choose a relatively powerful pump for a given size of pond. Submersible pumps, as their name suggests, are located below the water surface and are straightforward to set up. Surface-type pumps, although often having a greater capacity, must be housed in special surroundings close to the pond, in a position which is below the water level, and yet free from flooding.

Introducing Fish

As with aquaria, it is sensible to allow a week or so for the plants to start establishing themselves, before allowing fish into the pond. The best time to carry out the construction and stocking of a pond is late spring, when the dangers of severe weather are passed, and the plants should start to grow rapidly.

Veiltail

Red Cap Oranda

4 General Management

Goldfish are naturally omnivorous in their feeding habits, taking both livefood and vegetable matter as part of their diet in the wild. A range of straightforward substitute foods are now available, containing balanced amounts of carbohydrate, fat and protein with vitamins and minerals, for goldfish kept under artificial conditions. These are produced basically in the form of flakes or pellets, which must be stored in dry surroundings. A pelleted diet is ideal for pond fish, since it will attract them to the surface, as the pellets float. Flake foods are equally acceptable, however, although the flakes will only remain at the surface for a relatively short period before slowly sinking to the bottom. It is therefore easier to assess food consumption by using pellets for pond fish.

While goldfish will live well on a diet of this type alone, they often appear to do better if provided regularly with other items, such as livefood.

Livefood

Livefood is either aquatic or non-aquatic. Aquatic livefoods are mainly natural pond inhabitants and can introduce diseases to the fish as a result. Daphnia, also known as Water Fleas, are typical of this group, often being found in stagnant pools during summer, when they can be collected with a fine mesh net. These minute crustaceans which are not related to fleas, are also available from some aquatic stores. Any bags containing a large number of dead individuals are best avoided, and they must always be kept cool. Daphnia are thought to be a good conditioning food as well as being a laxative.

There is a constant danger when using aquatic livefoods that pests such as leeches may inadvertently be introduced along with the food itself. Special sieves for Daphnia are produced to minimise the risk, so that the water can be poured off, allowing the contents of the seive to be studied. Leeches appear as dark worm-like creatures.

Another useful crustacean, often occurring in the company of Daphnia, is Cyclops. Only a restricted number of such creatures should be fed at any time. They will absorb oxygen from the water like the fish, and an excessive number may deplete the concentration significantly, in a confined space such as an aquarium.

Another popular aquatic livefood, stocked by many dealers, is Tubifex. These are small worms which naturally live in mud and slime around such places as sewerage outflows. They may be sold wrapped in paper, but must be transferred back to water as soon as possible. Tubifex will survive well when kept in a shallow tray, covered with water. This will need to be changed at least daily and kept in a cool place out of direct sunlight. Small mats of these worms can be pulled off the main group with tweezers, and fed as necessary.

Other livefoods, which are not generally sold in their natural form, are more seasonal. These include bloodworms (*Chironomus*) and gnat larvae (*Culex*). The female midges and gnats can be attracted to lay their eggs by simply leaving a bucket of water outside during the summer. The larvae can then be sieved out once they hatch and fed to fish in aquaria.

Since the supply of livefood can be unpredictable, it is useful to have cultures established for use throughout the year and these are generally of non-aquatic origin. Whiteworm (*Enchytracus albidus*) starter cultures can be obtained either locally, or by mail order. An empty margarine tub with holes in the lid and filled with damp peat makes a very satisfactory pot for a small culture. Whiteworm feed on damp bread, which should be replaced every couple of days. They do best when kept in the dark in a temperature of 15°–20°C (58°–68°F), and can be easily removed by means of tweezers.

Grindal worms are similar in their requirements, but must be kept at about 21°C (70°F). Micro worms are slightly smaller, and therefore particularly good for young goldfish. Unfortunately, cultures go off quickly in this case, and new colonies need to be started about every five days, to ensure a constant supply without an offensive smell.

Earthworms can also be fed to goldfish, although they should be kept in dark, damp surroundings on grass for two or three days beforehand, to void their gut contents, which will otherwise soil the water. Depending on their size, earthworms may need to be cut up prior to feeding, which is an unpleasant task.

As an alternative, redworms (*Dendrobina rubica*) are generally smaller. Being popular as a coarse fishing bait, these worms can often be acquired from bait dealers, as well as aquarist shops.

Prepared Livefoods

It is also possible to purchase livefoods in a prepared form, and these are easy to store and use when needed. Freeze-dried tubifex for ex-

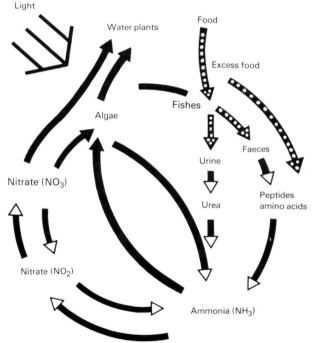

The nitrogen cycle:

The nitrogen cycle sees the degradation of toxic ammonia to less harmful compounds, notably nitrate which is used by algea and plants for their growth. Overfeeding fish will pollute the tank and overloads the cycle. The undergravel filter shows the cycle in operation.

ample, is simply fed by dropping an appropriate square on to the water's surface. Such items should not be confused with dried ants' eggs, which are of relatively little value.

Another development in fish nutrition is the growing number of gamma-irradiated frozen foods being produced. There is no risk of introducing disease with these items, and a variety of livefoods, such as tubifex and bloodworms are now being sold in this form. After opening, however, the foil packets must be kept in a refrigerator, and not re-frozen.

Various other foods can be offered to goldfish. Scrambled egg is popular, for example, while finely-cut cooked heart, with all fat removed, can also be used. To supplement their vegetable intake, a small amount of washed lettuce or boiled spinach may be given, while oatmeal is another possible alternative.

Feeding Principles

It is absolutely vital not to overfeed goldfish, particularly in an aquarium. Fish do not eat a lot at one time, but consume small amounts of food throughout the day. Too much food given all at once will rapidly sour the water, and thus only restricted quantities should be offered, with any surplus being removed if possible. Feeding will be necessary two or three times a day as a general rule, although the appetite of the fish is significantly influenced by the temperature of their surroundings.

Goldfish cease to feed once their water temperature falls below 4.4°C(40°F), and they become torpid, relying on their body fat stores to sustain them over such periods. It can be dangerous to feed fish under these conditions, because food will not be digested, and so remains in the gut, where it may start decomposing. At the onset of spring, as the water temperature rises again, the fish's appetite will return gradually. Goldfish in an aquarium are more likely to eat all the year round, since their water temperature will remain relatively constant, although there can be some fluctuations in their food intake. Their diet should show a seasonal change though if possible, with aquatic livefoods being fed when available. Such foods are a good conditioner for breeding purposes.

It is therefore quite possible for goldfish to be left safely over a holiday period of a fortnight or so without feeding. If, however, a friend or neighbour is caring for them, it will be vital to stress that only small amounts of food are required, and an excess may prove lethal.

Aquarium Maintenance

Once the tank is set up correctly, its maintenance requirements are minimal. At first though, algal growth can present difficulties until the lighting regime is sorted out. Green algae may develop rapidly on the sides of the aquarium, but can normally be removed using an aquarium scraper or just a clean cloth. Razor blades or similar sharp objects should not be used to clean algae from plastic tanks, as they are likely to damage the sides. When algae develop inside tubing, special brushes to clean them are available.

Regular maintenance of the aquarium will need to be carried out every two or three weeks. Apart from removing excess algae, it will be necessary to change up to one third of the water. This can be baled out carefully, using a clean vessel, although in order to remove any accumulated debris from the floor of the aquarium, a means of syphoning will be necessary. A length of rubber tubing, such as a bunsen burner lead, is ideal used in conjunction with a bucket below the level of the tank.

Fill the tubing with water, and then cover each end with a finger and place in the aquarium and the bucket respectively. By releasing the finger over the end in the aquarium first, water will flow from the tank into the bucket when the other finger is removed. Mulm which has collected on the gravel can be simply removed by this means, taking care not to suck up too much gravel at the same time otherwise this will block the water flow. The suction force generated at the end of the tube can be quite powerful, so the goldfish must always be kept away from it, to avoid possible injury.

Matured tapwater can then be introduced to the tank by the same means, if the bucket is positioned higher than the aquarium. Alternatively, it can be gently poured in from a container, to make the level up to its original depth.

Within the tank itself, rockwork may need to be removed and scrubbed free of algae. Any ailing plants will have to be taken out and replaced and any excessive growth must be curtailed. As an occasional fertiliser, some

Bubble-Eye

Golden Orfe

aquarists place a rabbit or guinea pig dropping under the gravel close to the plants.

While an undergravel filter will not need any maintenance unless its pores become blocked by plant roots, box filters must be cleaned out as mentioned previously. Every six months or so, the pump itself will also need to be over-hauled, and its rubber diaphragm replaced. Most pumps are sold with spare diaphragms, and it is a relatively simple task to change this component.

Pond Maintenance

Ponds also require a certain amount of main-tenance to keep them looking attractive throughout the year. They will benefit from being cleaned out at least annually, to remove the debris which will have accumulated at the bottom. This task can be carried out either in the early spring or during the autumn.

5 Health

Correct management of the goldfish will do much to prevent outbreaks of disease. Parasitic afflictions are relatively common, but sensible precautions such as quarantining new fish, washing plants and screening livefood will do much to keep such pests at bay. They will obviously be harder to eliminate from a pond, where it may also prove more difficult to actually spot an ailing fish until it is seriously ill. Feeding time provides an ideal opportunity to look at the fish though and note any that appear to be slightly off-colour. If they then show no improvement, they must be caught and placed in an isolation tank.

Poisons

There are cases, however, when all the fish will appear distressed, often as a result of overcrowding or poisoning. Under these circumstances, they are likely to be seen gulping at the surface. Under pond conditions, certain plants, notably holly, laburnum and rhododendron will poison fish should their leaves or seeds fall into the water. Insecticides and weedkillers are generally harmful, and must never be used close to a pond. In the home, many aerosols are poisonous to fish, and care needs to be taken to cover the tank completely if they have to be used. The air-borne particles will remain in suspension for a period after the actual spraying is completed, so the aquarium must not be uncovered immediately. There is little specific treatment available for poisoning, apart from moving the fish at once to an uncontaminated environment, where hopefully, they will recover.

Particular Signs to Note

When ill, fish often have difficulty in swimming, and their buoyancy may be affected. In certain instances, they may rub themselves on rockwork, giving rise to sore or inflamed areas on their bodies. This behaviour is often seen in conjunction with skin irritations. The eyes also may become clouded or swollen as a result of various ailments. Indeed, combinations of diseases are quite common. Parasitic and fungal infections for example, will frequently occur together, as one lowers the resistance of the fish to the other.

Treatments

Treatment of fish diseases is now relatively straightforward, as effective proprietary remedies can be bought from most aquarist stores. These must be used as directed, and on no account should an excessive dose be given, as this is highly likely to have adverse, rather than beneficial, effects. Antibiotics are now being used increasingly in fish medicine but these can only be obtained on veterinary prescription in Britain. When faced with severe outbreaks of disease, it will be worth having post-mortems carried out at a specialist laboratory. Contact with such institutions can be made through a veterinarian.

Digestive Disorders

The most common cause of digestive disorders is feeding excessive dry food over a long period of time. Constipation itself is evident by trailing of dropping while the fish is swimming. The remedy is to provide a more varied diet, including Daphnia which have a laxative effect.

Dropsy

This is a symptom, rather than a specific disease in itself. The fish's belly swells up over a period of time, and other changes such as exophthalmia, which distorts the eyes, may also be evident. Possible causes include infections by bacteria and viruses, and whereas the former may respond to antibiotics, there is no effective treatment for viral disease, and the fish will have to be destroyed.

Eye Disease

The most alarming condition affecting one or both eyes is described as 'pop eye'. The diseased eye swells up, and may ultimately be forced out of its socket, although this does not appear to cause the fish much discomfort. There is no single cause of pop eye, or exophthalmia as it is otherwise known, and hence a successful cure cannot be guaranteed.

Opacity of the lens, or cataract, will give the eye a whitish appearance. In some cases, larval worms are responsible. They will have hatched in the water before burrowing into the fish, and migrating to the eye. Treatment is not always possible.

Fin Rot

This complaint is most commonly seen in varieties with well-developed finnage. The edges of the fins become ragged and have an uneven appearance, often most noticeable .in the caudal fin. Fin rot is of bacterial origin, although a fungal infection may develop almost simultaneously. It generally occurs in fish kept in overcrowded, dirty conditions. Proprietary remedies from an aquarist store can be used for treatment, or antibiotics. Affected fish should always be treated in a separate tank. Antibiotics dissolved in the water are liable to destroy the beneficial bacteria associated with an undergravel filter, while other remedies may even discolour the tank sealant. Fin rot can be fatal, so early action will give the best chance of a successful recovery.

Fungal Disease

Fungal infections attack weakened or diseased fish. The spores of the fungi can be commonly isolated from most tanks and ponds, and yet no evidence of disease normally exists in the fish themselves. Fungal growth will give fish a patchy whitish appearance rather reminiscent of cotton wool. Once again, proprietary treatments are available, or salt baths, using 28 grams of salt to 4.5 litres of water (1 oz to 1 gallon) should overcome the infection. Affected fish must be given plenty of livefood to help them recover.

Parasites

A wide range of parasites can affect goldfish, and the aim must be to keep these out of the aquarium or pond by careful management, rather than having to treat any resulting disease.

Perhaps the most significant parasite is *Ichthyopthirius*, often abbreviated to 'Ich' or 'Ick', which is the protozoa responsible for causing white spot. It spends only part of its life cycle embedded in the fish's skin, giving rise to the characteristic white spots over the whole body. Once mature, it falls off and divides on the bottom of the aquarium or pond. Here it can give rise to as many as a thousand immature free-swimming intermediates called tomites. These must then find a fish to complete the cycle, or else they will die after several days. Obviously within the confines of an aquarium in particular, a severe outbreak of 'Ich' can occur rapidly.

The fish will be severely weakened, and may well succumb to fungal infections if they do not actually die beforehand. Commercial remedies will overcome this parasite, but it can be a lengthy process, with not all treatments being active against the parasite when it is embedded in the skin.

The female Anchor Worm (*Lernaea*) will actually bore into the fish's body, where ultimately she dies, having laid her eggs. *Lernaea* has a thread-like appearance, and may reach 1.9 cm ($\frac{3}{4}$ in) in length. The best treatment is to dab the wound with potassium permanganate solution, which will kill the parasite. Then as the fish still lies restrained in a wet net, the Anchor Worm can be pulled out carefully with tweezers. The site of attachment should finally be dabbed with iodine solution. In a pond, it will take two months to eliminate the parasite from the water once all the fish are removed.

The Fish Louse (Argulus) is related to the Anchor Worm, and also attacks fish, sucking their blood. It has a flattish appearance, and often occurs in the company of Daphnia. Similar treatment will destroy it.

Flukes are another parasite that may attach to the skin. They are very small in appearance, and thus hard to spot as a result. They will however, cause the skin to take on a slimy appearance and blood spots may also be evident. Gill flukes will cause the fish to have difficulty in breathing, actually destroying the gill tissue itself. A 3 per cent salt solution will overcome these parasites. Leeches in contrast are not actually killed by salt but will be dislodged from the skin, after the fish has been immersed in the solution for a quarter of an hour or so.

The foregoing gives a brief list of the most common parasites encountered on goldfish. Within a pond however, there will be a variety of other predatory creatures which are likely to attack the fish, particularly young specimens. While Water Boatmen for example are totally aquatic, and thus should be relatively easy to exclude, others, such as alder fly larvae present more of a threat, as the adult fly lays its eggs directly in water. Even if these creatures do not actually destroy the fish, they can injure them sufficiently to enable infections to develop which kill the fish.

6 **Breeding**

Goldfish are not difficult fish to breed successfully, and the development of the fry is a fascinating process to observe at close quarters. Enthusiasts aiming to produce goldfish for exhibition purposes will invariably use tanks, so that the pedigree of the resulting fish is controlled, and their rearing can be closely supervised. In ponds, the breeding of goldfish is a much more haphazard affair, and far fewer fry will ultimately survive.

Breeding Condition

A certain degree of preparation is essential to bring the fish into top condition. A good supply of livefood is recommended, with chopped earthworm regarded as perhaps the best conditioner by many aquarists. Under natural conditions, it appears that a rise in water temperature also stimulates breeding, and therefore spring is the best time for success.

When goldfish come into breeding condition, males can be recognised by the white pimples on their gill plates, which may extend up to the foremost part of the pectoral fins. This should not be confused with the parasite affliction known as white spot, covered in the previous chapter. Females swell with eggs prior to spawning, although this characteristic is not so noticeable in the more fancy varieties, with their shortened, corpulent bodies. Both sexes swim more forcibly, while males will be seen nudging at prospective mates.

Spawning Set-up

For most satisfactory results, goldfish should be confined in a special spawning tank. Unfortunately they will eat their eggs immediately after laying if given an opportunity, and although obviously some will survive and hatch under pond conditions, the chances of young fish being reared in an aquarium alongside their parents are very low.

A tank for spawning purposes does not need to be an elaborate set-up, although it should be as large as possible, preferably 90 cm (3 ft) in length. Plants or an artificial spawning mop will be needed at one end, where the female will lay her eggs. Once the water has matured, the male should be transferred into the tank during the evening, with the female being introduced about a day later. After nudging the female, the male will then start to chase her more aggressively, driving her towards the plants or mop where the eggs will be deposited.

Fertilisation is effected by the male as the eggs are laid. They are minute at first, but rapidly take up water and swell, appearing pale yellow in colour. They are naturally adhesive, and will stick readily to the spawning medium, or even the sides of the tank. Once the fish have finished spawning, they must be removed from the aquarium. Occasionally, those with long fins may have damaged themselves in the heat of the chase, and such injuries should be watched carefully, to ensure that no infection develops. Fish when spawning are also especially at risk from predators, since they lose their normal caution. This is of particular importance with pond fish, since neighbourhood cats can then gain an unexpected meal without difficulty.

If the fish do not spawn immediately, they should be left together for a few days. It is generally not recommended to feed them during this period, because of the risk of contaminating the water. Fry are particularly susceptible to polluted water. Since fish appear to be stimulated to spawn by shafts of sunlight falling on their water in the morning, the tank, if possible, should be placed in a suitable position for this purpose.

Hatching of the Eggs

It is common practice to heat the tank where the eggs are developing to a temperature in the range 21°–25°C (70°–75°F), which will reduce the hatching period to between three and four days, with no adverse effects. A higher temperature will result in sickly fry. A simple aquarium heater connected to a thermostat should be used for the purpose, with a combined unit being most straightforward. A thermometer, to monitor the water temperature, will also be required, and the apparatus should be tested before being introduced to the spawning tank. Any eggs which are infertile turn whitish, and will ultimately be attacked by fungus. Although it is not essential to remove these, it is preferable, to reduce unnecessary fungal growth in a tank containing young fish.

At a temperature of 10°C (50°F), as in a pond, the fry may not hatch for two weeks or so, and are very vulnerable at this stage. In order to ensure that some survive, the female goldfish will lay at least 500 eggs at a time. While males can be used for breeding when a year old, females in their second year generally give better results and can spawn three times a year. They may continue breeding for a decade or more, although obviously fewer fry can be expected when using old fish.

When the fry first hatch, they will be inactive and simply fix themselves in amongst the plants or on the aquarium glass. Any disturbance then is likely to be fatal for them, since their air-bladders, which ultimately provide buoyancy, are only just developing. They do not eat at this stage, being sustained by the remnants of their yolk sacs. Within two days of hatching, they will be free-swimming, and consuming food avidly. Young goldfish eat a huge amount of food relative to their size.

While it is relatively easy to spawn goldfish, for this reason the rearing period is most challenging. Infusoria is the traditional first food given to fry. It is made up of various unicellular creatures, which develop in water containing decomposing vegetable matter. Cultures should therefore be set up before spawning, by placing crushed lettuce leaves in a large jar full of water, preferably with the addition of some aquarium water, which will already contain these minute organisms. They will rapidly multiply under such conditions in a warm environment, and several jars should be started in succession, to ensure a constant supply.

The infusoria are then fed through a continuous drip feed into the tank containing the fry. This is achieved by using a piece of narrow bore air piping with a clamp to regulate the flow rate. The flow in this case can be started by sucking one end of the pipe, while the other is kept in the jar containing the infusoria. This will, of course, have to be placed higher than the tank itself.

Various other alternative foods for fry are marketed commercially, and will be more reliable than preparing infusoria. In addition, Brine Shrimp (Artemia) cultures, although relatively expensive to prepare, give good results. Detailed instructions are included with each pack, but only a relatively small quantity should be purchased at any time. Once exposed to the air, the eggs rapidly deteriorate, and the hatchability is adversely affected as a result. Open packs must always be kept in air-tight containers. Brine Shrimp eggs have to be hatched in salt water, which is both heated and well-aerated. The larvae, referred to as *nauplii*, emerge within a day, and can then be sieved out and given to the fry.

As the young fish reach a month old, other items such as small Daphnia can be used to replace the nauplii in their diet. Hard-boiled egg, forced through muslin to ensure that only fine particles are on offer, is a useful standby if faced with a shortage of livefoods. Unfortunately egg will cloud the water extremely rapidly, and so must be given in very small quantities. Larger items, such as chopped whiteworm, can then be introduced to the growing fry after Daphnia.

Under aquarium conditions, very many fry

should survive, but it is unlikely that it will be possible to rear all these. Insufficient food and space will lead to a large number of poor fish being produced, and so as a first step, any obviously malformed or stunted individuals should be removed. They can, if desired, be fed to the adult fish and will have a quick end under these circumstances.

Development of the Fry

By the age of six weeks, it will be possible to distinguish the scale types of the young goldfish. Nacreous fish do not breed true, so that proportions of their offspring will be matt and metallic, as well as nacreous. Goldfish of these two former types, when paired together, yield fry which are exclusively nacreous in appearance.

When transferring fry into other tanks, great care is needed. It is preferable to catch them using a ladle, since a net will injure them at this stage. The temperature of their new surroundings must correspond closely to the water where they were being kept previously. Gradually though, the temperature of their water should be reduced so that eventually it falls down to an unheated level.

In the case of pond varieties then, fish which were hatched in tanks early in the year and have attained a size of at least 5 cm (2 ins) can be overwintered successfully outside, having been acclimatised as necessary. Young goldfish transferred to ponds must never be kept alongside larger individuals though, because cannabilism will be quite common under these circumstances.

As the goldfish develop, so their characteristic features will become increasingly evident. Protuberant eyes, associated with certain varieties such as the Moor, are not evident until the fry are at least three months of age. They should possess telescope-eyes, whereas the Celestial will have upturned eyes following a telescope-eyed stage in its development. Such fish are not handicapped by their poor vision in a tank alongside counterparts with normal eyes, since they locate food primarily by their sense of smell. Some individuals may only develop one protuberant eye, and are therefore normally culled.

Fish diseases:
This diagram shows some of the common ailments which fish may succumb. A number are parasitic in origin and can be introduced to an aquarium by new fish, plants and live food.
Other ailments results from poor management.

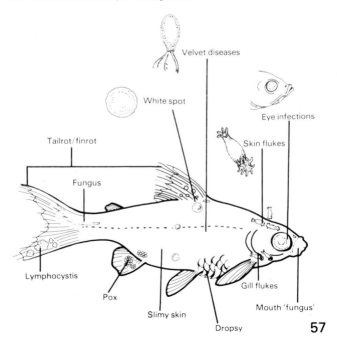

Velvet diseases

White spot

Eye infections

Tailrot/finrot

Skin flukes

Fungus

Lymphocystis

Pox

Gill flukes

Slimy skin

Mouth 'fungus'

Dropsy

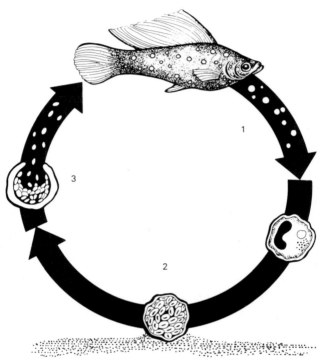

How White-spot disease is spread:
1. White spots are evident on the fish's body.
2. Parasites then spread forming cysts at the bottom of the aquarium.
3. These then give use to a free-swimming stage which infects the fish again.

7 A Selection of Other Coldwater Fish

Although the goldfish in its many forms remains the most popular of the coldwater fishes, there are others that can be kept both in ponds and aquaria without difficulty. Such fish are listed in this chapter.

Carp

The carp belonging to the genus *Cyprinus* are related to goldfish, but can be distinguished by the presence of fleshy protrusions known as barbels at the corners of their mouths. The Common Carp in fact has a similar history of domestication to that of the goldfish, being valued at first both for food and its attractive coloration. The most unusual variety that has since been developed is the Mirror Carp, named after the striking reflective scales running down the sides of its body, which are greatly enlarged in size. A much duller form, known as the Leather Carp, is also seen for sale on occasions. These fish can grow quite large when kept under favourable conditions, and are easy to look after. When small, they can be housed quite satisfactorily in an aquarium, but as they get bigger, a pond will provide a more suitable environment for them. Their barbels are thought to have a sensory function, enabling the fish to detect food in murky water, and they may disturb the substrate of the aquarium in the search for particles of food.

A distinctive colour form of the Common Carp has become known as the Hi Goi, being developed in Japan from Chinese stock. It is yellowish in appearance. Small specimens, generally under 10 cm (4 ins) in length, are frequently available, but bear in mind that these fish can grow as large as 50 cm (20 ins), although often they will not attain this size, even under pond conditions. It may well be preferable to keep young fish in an aquarium over the winter months, so they will continue feeding, and grow more rapidly as a result.

Undoubtedly however, the Koi Carp are the most popular members of this particular group of fish. Their origins are unclear, and interbreeding with goldfish may have occurred in the past, since not all koi have the barbels characteristic of their *Cyprinus* ancestors. Large koi make spectacular pond occupants, frequently growing over 30 cm (12 ins), while smaller fish will be attractive occupants of a large aquarium. The domestication of the koi, and the spectacular array of scale types and colours now seen, began in Japan. Prize specimens sell for vast sums of money, but a good selection of small koi are stocked by many pet stores and garden centres at moderate prices, with the largest selection being available in the summer months. During recent years, the large American fish-farms that produce goldfish for the trade have also started breeding koi, and these fish are generally cheaper than their more illustrious Japanese counterparts.

The scale types of koi can be divided into four basic categories. Some fish have scales like those of Mirror Carp following hybridisation, whereas other koi are significantly brighter in their overall coloration. A matt variety, which is dull in comparison, as well as an intermediate form can also be obtained, in a range of colours. Since becoming popular in the West, the characteristic names of koi have not been altered from the original Japanese descriptions. This can give rise to confusion, but does not in any way detract from the individual beauty of these fish. Whereas goldfish have been bred with regard to developments of their fins and body, koi carp are remarkably uniform in their overall appearance having been developed for their coloration.

One of the most popular colour combinations today is the red and white form, known as *Kohaku*, while the pure golden *Ohgan* reveals how single-coloured fish can be equally striking. Indeed, the Japanese name for these fish, *Nishikigoi*, means Colourful Carp. The description 'koi' has arisen from the Japanese word for carp, which is 'goi'. Many of these fish are still known by their Japanese names.

Other colour forms are recognised, with koi showing one, two or even three different colours on their bodies. In most instances, the colour does not fade as the fish gets older, although exceptions such as the metallic gold Kinsui are known. During recent years, the so-called Ghost Koi, with narrow golden stripes and fins set against a dark body colour have become very popular.

Koi carp can grow to 60 cm (2 ft) in length, and need suitably spacious surroundings. Indeed, if they are to be kept in a pond, it will have to be planned very much with their needs in mind, as these fish are unsuitable for the average small garden pond. This is not only because of their size and active natures. In order to be fully appreciated, they must be kept in relatively clear water, which will necessitate the use of a filter, especially during the summer months, when algae will develop rapidly and cloud the pond. Koi are also destructive fish, and may uproot plants, as well as eating them, so that it can be difficult to include them in a semi-natural setting. If you want to keep the fish outside through the winter, the pond will have to be quite deep, with about 1.2 m (4 ft) being the minimum for this purpose. It may also be advisable to invest in a pond heater, to prevent the whole of the water's surface freezing over, restricting the environment of the fish, so that gases cannot enter and leave the water as would normally happen, polluting their environment instead. Koi are easy to feed however, on a standard diet of pellets, and may even become sufficiently trusting to feed almost directly from the hand. Under ideal conditions, these fish will grow very rapidly, so do allow for this when stocking the pond initially, and avoid filling it to its maximum capacity at this stage. Breeding habits closely resemble those of the goldfish.

Catfish

Another group of fish characterised by barbels close to their mouths are the catfish, which

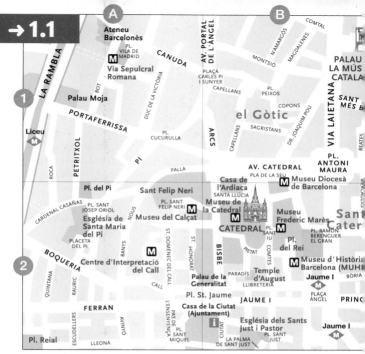

A magnet for artists in the early 20th century. Catalan cuisine.

IRATI TAVERNA VASCA
Cardenal Casañas, 17
→1.1 A2
T 93 302 30 84
(30-50 €)
One of BCN's first Basque restaurants. Tapas.

KOY SHUNKA
Copons, 7 →1.1 B1
T 93 412 49 91
(50-60 €) + TASTING MENU
Japanese haute cuisine with a Catalan twist.

SELF NATURISTA
Santa Anna, 11 →1.3 B1
T 93 318 26 84
(10-20 €) + SET LUNCH MENU
One of Barcelona's first vegetarian restaurants. Self-service, 11am-8pm.

Cafés and bars
BAR DEL PI
Pl. Sant Josep Oriol, 1
→1.1 A2
Café and tapas bar with a wonderful terrace where you can savour the atmos-

phere of the neighbourhood.

BODEGA LA PALMA
La Palma de Sant Just, 7
→1.1 B2
A traditional bodega serving excellent omelettes and Catalan cured meats and sausage.

CAELUM
Palla, 8 →1.1 A2
Shop selling products from different convents. Café on the premises where you can sample them.

EL MESÓN DEL CAFÉ
Llibreteria, 16 →1.1 B2
Since 1909. The current décor dates from 1929. Tiny bar serving great coffee.

EL PARAIGÜA
Pas de l'Ensenyança, 2
→1.1 A2
Historic cocktail bar and café. *Modernista* décor. Live music. Exhibitions.

LA GRANJA
Banys nous, 4 →1.1 A2
A café since 1872, it retains all its charm. The interior

houses a section of the Roman wall.

GRANJA LA PALLARESA
Petritxol, 11 →1.1 A1
Serving one of the best thick hot chocolates in the city since 1947.

Shops
ARTUR RAMON
Palla, 10 →1.1 A2
One of Barcelona's finest antique shops, now run by the fourth generation of the same family.

BCN ORIGINAL
Ciutat, 2 →1.3 B2
Pl. Catalunya, 7→1.3 B1
A wide range of gift items inspired by Barcelona.

CERERIA SUBIRÀ
Llibreteria, 7 →1.1 B2
The finest candles since 1761. Baroque décor.

DEULOFEU 1918
Call, 30 →1.1 A2
100 years dressing the people of Barcelona in the latest fashions.

GANIVETERIA ROCA
Pl. del Pi, 3 →1.1 A2

El Born + La Ribera

La Ribera — meaning shore — bears witness to the city's former relationship with the sea. La Ribera was built in the 13th century outside the city walls and partially demolished to make way for a military citadel which was later turned into a park. It still retains its higgledy-piggledy medieval layout where Santa Maria del Mar, El Born, and the Santa Caterina Market stand out like clearings in a dense forest.

Barcelona Walking Tours
Picasso
Two-hour walking tour led by professional guides exploring the life and work of the painter during the time he spent in Barcelona. The tour includes Els Quatre Gats, the Col·legi d'Arquitectes, the Sala Parés, Carrer Escudellers Blancs, Carrer Avinyó, Carrer de la Plata, the Porxos d'En Xifré, Llotja de Mar, La Ribera district and ends at the Museu Picasso. Price: adults, 19,50 €; children, 7 € (includes guided visit of Museu Picasso). Times: Tuesday, Thursday and Saturday, 16 noon (English); Saturday, 16 noon (Catalan and Spanish). Departs from the Turisme de Barcelona Information Office (Pl. Catalunya, 17-s).

Museums
MUSEU BARBIER-MUELLER D'ART PRECOLOMBÍ
Montcada, 14 →1.2 B3
www.barbier-mueller.ch
One of Europe's most prestigious collections of art from America's pre-Hispanic cultures.

DISSENY HUB BARCELONA
Montcada, 12 →1.2 B3
www.dhub-bcn.cat
Temporary home of this group of design and decorative arts museums. It hosts exhibitions from its permanent collection at its headquarters in Pedralbes.

MUSEU DE LA XOCOLATA
Comerç, 36 →1.2 B2
www.pastisseria.cat
A journey tracing the origins of chocolate, its arrival in Europe and widespread use.

Restaurants

More than 60 € → P. 88
COMERÇ 24 *
SAUC *
EL PASSADÍS D'EN PEP

* Michelin-starred

CAL PEP
Pl. de les Olles, 8 →1.2 B3
T 93 310 79 61
(40-50 €)
Very popular. Home cooking with a Basque flavour and excellent tapas.

CUINES DE SANTA CATERINA
Av. Francesc Cambó, 16 →1.2 A2. T 93 268 99 18
(20-40 €)
Modern and spacious. Inside the Santa Caterina Market. Mediterranean, oriental and vegetarian cuisine.

SENYOR PARELLADA
Argenteria, 37 →1.2 A3
T 93 310 50 94
(25-40 €)
Charming restaurant. Generous servings of traditional Catalan cuisine.

Cafés and bars
GIMLET
Rec, 24 →1.2 B3
Classic 1970's cocktail bar paying tribute to Raymond Chandler. Jazz.

LA VINYA DEL SENYOR
Pl. Santa Maria, 5 →1.2 A3
A wide selection of wines to accompany tasting dishes of Catalan cured sausage, ham, cheese...

MIRAMELINDO
Pg. del Born, 15 →1.2 B3
Soft lighting and music and a warm atmosphere. The ideal place for a good cocktail.

PITIN BAR
Pg. del Born, 34 →1.2 B3
The oldest bar in the neighbourhood. Cosy and charming.

Shops
BUBÓ
Caputxes, 10 →1.2 A3
Mampel, the world's top chocolatier in 2005, offers us his modern creations.

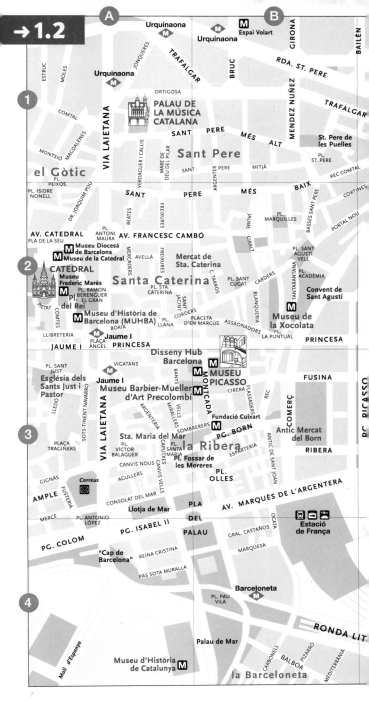

La Rambla

There's no street in Barcelona like La Rambla: an explosion of life and colour which attracts people of all countries and backgrounds. La Rambla is the dividing line between the Gothic Quarter and El Raval: a broad pedestrian walkway, bustling with people night and day, which links the Mediterranean with the Eixample. It is lined with news-stands and flower stalls.

Barcelona Walking Tours
Gourmet

Two-hour walking tour led by professional guides exploring Barcelona's culinary culture. Visit the Granja Viader, the Boqueria Market, the patisserie Escribà, Caelum, La Colmena and the Santa Caterina Market. Price: adults, 19,50 €; children, 7 € (includes two tastings). Times: Friday and Saturday, 10.00am (English); Saturday, 10.30am (Catalan and Spanish). Departs from the Turisme de Barcelona Information Office (Plaça Catalunya, 17-s).

Museums

ARTS SANTA MÒNICA
Rambla Santa Mònica, 7
→ **1.3** A4
www.artssantamonica.cat
A space of convergence and crossover between the different disciplines of contemporary artistic creation and science, thought and communication.

LA VIRREINA
CENTRE DE LA IMATGE
La Rambla, 99 → **1.3** A2
www.bcn.cat/virreinacentredelaimatge
Two gallery spaces devoted to pioneering visual arts.

MUSEU DE CERA
Passatge de la Banca, 7
→ **1.3** A4
www.museocerabcn.com
Some of the most eminent

figures in history come to life in a Renaissance-style building.

Restaurants

AGUT
Gignàs, 16 → **1.3** B4
T 93 315 17 09
(25-40 €) + SET LUNCH MENU
A former inn (1924) with a bohemian atmosphere. Excellent traditional Catalan cuisine.

ATTIC
La Rambla, 120 → **1.3** B2
T 93 302 48 66
(25-35 €) + GROUP MENU
Mediterranean cuisine with its own personal style. Views of La Rambla.

BAR LOBO
Pintor Fortuny, 3 → **1.3** A2
T 93 481 53 46
(20-30 €) + SET LUNCH MENU
Tapas and quick bites with a bold touch.

CAN CULLERETES
Quintana, 5 → **1.3** A3
T 93 317 30 22
(20-30 €) + GROUP MENU
Barcelona's oldest restaurant (1786). Traditional Catalan fare.

CENT ONZE
La Rambla, 111 → **1.3** B1
T 93 316 46 60
(30-50 €) + SET LUNCH MENU
French and Catalan tradition in a magnificent setting.

EGIPTE
La Rambla, 79 → **1.3** A2
T 93 317 95 45
(15-20 €) + SET LUNCH MENU
Traditional Catalan cuisine offering good value for money.

LOS CARACOLES
Escudellers, 14 → **1.3** A3
T 93 302 31 85
(30-45 €) + TAPAS MENU
Historic restaurant (1835). Simple, traditional Catalan cuisine.

PINOTXO
Mercat de la Boqueria
→ **1.3** A2
T 93 317 17 31
(20-30 €)
Small, famous bar inside the Boqueria Market. Dishes of the day and sandwiches.

TAXIDERMISTA
Pl. Reial, 8 → **1.3** A3
T 93 412 45 36
(30-45 €) + SET LUNCH MENU
Market-fresh and Mediterranean cuisine in a 19th-century building with minimalist décor.

Cafés and bars

BOADAS
Tallers, 1 → **1.3** B1
The Barcelona cocktail bar (1933). Classic décor and excellent cocktails.

CAFÈ DE L'ÒPERA
La Rambla, 74 → **1.3** A3
Legendary city café. It still has its mid-19th-century décor.

ESCRIBÀ
La Rambla, 83 → **1.3** A2
Café located in a patisserie founded over 100 years ago. You simply have to try its cakes and pastries.

SCHILLING
Ferran, 23 → **1.3** B3
Minimalist but cosy café. Open until 3am.

Highlights

→ 1.3 A3
GRAN TEATRE DEL LICEU
La Rambla, 51-59
T 93 485 99 00
www.liceubarcelona.com
Barcelona's opera house has experienced many changes in fortune: memorable performances (featuring Montserrat Caballé, Josep Carreras and Jaume Aragall, to name just three), fights between Verdi supporters and Wagnerians, and two major fires. It was renovated and extended following the fire in 1994.

Gran Teatre del Liceu **→ 1.3** A3

→ 1.3 A2
MERCAT DE SANT JOSEP «LA BOQUERIA»
Pl. de la Boqueria, s/n
T 93 318 25 84
www.boqueria.info
La Boqueria is Barcelona's best-stocked and most colourful food market. Under its shady metal structure, the stallholders sell an exquisite selection of fresh produce – meat, fish, fruit, vegetables – in a bustling, vibrant setting. ➕ p. 53

La Boqueria **→ 1.3** A2

→ 1.3 A3
PLAÇA REIAL
Barcelona's great porticoed square is made particularly outstanding by its rectilinear layout, tall palm trees, Gaudiesque street lamps and sunny terraces. It brings together bars, restaurants and music venues, hosting flamenco and jazz performances.

Plaça Reial **→ 1.3** A3

→ 1.3 A3
PALAU GÜELL
Nou de la Rambla, 3-5
T 93 472 57 75
www.palauguell.cat
This Gaudí landmark is defined by its majestic air which is expressed in its façade and large drawing room with its domed roof which lets in natural light. Its rooftop contains 20 chimneys with cowls covered in multicoloured ceramics. ➕ p. 54

Palau Güell **→ 1.3** A3

VIENA
La Rambla, 115 → **1.3** B1
Beer served in ceramic
tankards. Top-quality
sandwiches. Fast food
Catalan style.

ZURICH
Pl. Catalunya, 1 → **1.3** B1
A meeting place for locals
for 80 years.

Shops
CASA GIMENO
La Rambla, 100 → **1.3** A4
The world's finest tobacco
since 1920.

CASAS
La Rambla, 125 → **1.3** A2
Shoe retailers since 1923.
The top footwear collec-
tions and latest trends.

CUSTO BARCELONA
Ferran, 36 → **1.3** B3
Everything in men's and
women's fashion by BCN's
top international designer.

DOCUMENTA
Cardenal Casañas, 4
→ **1.3** A2
One of Barcelona's best
bookshops. Opened in
1975.

FELGAR
La Rambla, 132 → **1.3** B1
Ladies' fashions and
accessories.

HERBORISTERIA
DEL REI
Vidre, 1 → **1.3** A3
Since 1823. Décor dating
from 1860. The oldest
herbalist's in Catalonia.

SANTA RITA
Doctor Dou, 11 → **1.3** A1
A selection of books, music
and unusual gift items.

And also
EL INGENIO
Rauric, 6 → **1.3** B3
Since 1838. Creating
products associated
with fun, games and
entertainment as well
as papier-mâché figures
(giants and big heads).

PLAÇA DE LA MERCÈ
→ **1.3** B4
Named after the church of
La Mercè, which dates from
1775. The square features
an imposing fountain
depicting Neptune.

Information Point → **1.1**A3

Canaletes Fountain → **1.3** B1

Pla de l'Os → **1.3**A2

Church of La Mercè → **1.3** B4

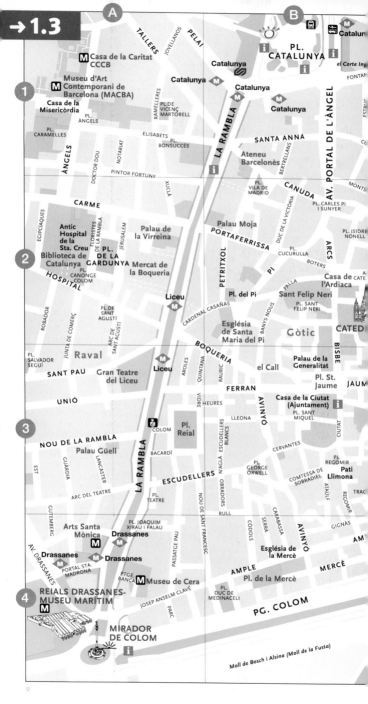

El Raval

El Raval is a laboratory for the Barcelona of the future. For years, it was marked by neglect and the shabby Barrio Chino, but today it is a constantly evolving gateway to the city, the home to communities of different nationalities, and a place where culture, retail and leisure activities converge. The splendid Rambla del Raval now presides over the traditional heart of the neighbourhood.

Art galleries

Since the MACBA and CCCB opened, a wide variety of galleries and design shops have come here to complement a cultural offering which was practically non-existent a decade ago. Most of them are places where cutting-edge artists from around the world exhibit their works, meet up and exchange views. Below you will find a short list of these premises, but we recommend you take a leisurely stroll in order to discover the vitality of this Barcelona neighbourhood. Foment de les Arts Decoratives, FAD, (Pl. dels Àngels, 5-6, www.fadweb. org); Cotthem Gallery (Dr. Dou, 15, www.cotthem. com); Galeria Ferran Cano (Pl. Duc de Medinaceli, 6, www.artnet.com); Àngels Barcelona (Pintor Fortuny, 27, www.angelsbarcelona. com); Tinta Invisible (Lleó, 6); Cafè Nou 3 (Dr. Dou, 12); Antidoto28 (Ferlandina, 28, www. vorticedesign.net); Taller Obert (Ferlandina, 49); Holala! Gallery (Valldonzella, 4).

Restaurants

More than 60 € → P. 88
CASA LEOPOLDO

FÀBRICA MORITZ
Ronda Sant Antoni, 41
→ **1.4** A1
T 93 423 54 34
A huge leisure, dining and cultural complex which is home to a beer hall and restaurant.
CAN LLUÍS
Cera, 49 → **1.4** A2
T 93 441 11 87
(20-30 €) + SET LUNCH MENU
A Raval classic. Family atmosphere. Catalan home cooking.
DOS PALILLOS
Elisabets, 9 → **1.4** C1
T 93 304 05 13
(30-40 €) + TASTING MENU
Asian haute-cuisine tapas and excellent sakes, wines, beers and teas.
FONDA ESPAÑA
Sant Pau, 9-11 → **1.4** C3
T 93 318 17 58
Catalan cuisine in a *modernista* dining room by Domènech i Montaner. Junta de Comerç, 11
ORGÀNIC
→ **1.4** B2. T 93 301 09 02
(15-20 €) + SET LUNCH MENU
Large and quiet dining room. Vegetarian cuisine with biological food.

Cafés and bars

Don't forget the city's classics, including **Marsella, 1820,** (Sant Pau, 65); **Almirall**, 1860, (Joaquín Costa, 33) and the **London Bar, 1910,** (Nou de la Rambla, 34), once frequented by Picasso, Dalí and Hemingway.

BAR CAÑETE
Unió, 17 → **1.4** B3
T 93 358 84 41
(10-20 €) + SET LUNCH MENU
The former Bar Orgía, one of the typical neighbourhood bars, reopens as an informal restaurant where you can eat at the bar. Specialises in tapas.
BAR KASPARO
Pl Vicenç Martorell, 4→ **1.4** C1
A classic pavement café. Breakfasts, snacks, tapas...
GRANJA VIADER
Xuclà, 6 → **1.4** C2
Opened as a dairy in 1904. Delicious thick hot chocolate, topped with whipped cream and honeys, curd cheese, etc.
ORXATERIA SIRVENT
Parlament, 56 → **1.4** A2
In summer, people from all over town make a pilgrimage to Sirvent for an *orxata*, a milky drink made from tiger nuts.
RAVAL BAR
Doctor Dou, 19 → **1.4** B1
Drinks.

Shops
BHUNO
Elisabets, 18 → **1.4** C1
Original, exclusive clothes by cutting-edge Spanish designers.
BARCELONA REYKJAVIK
Doctor Dou, 12 → **1.4** B1
Hand-crafted bread made from ancient Nordic recipes using organic ingredients.

Highlights

→ **1.4** B1
MACBA
Plaça del Àngels, 1
T 93 412 08 10
www.macba.cat
The Museu d'Art
Contemporani de Barcelona,
one of the world's foremost
art museums, is housed in a
light, airy building designed
by Richard Meier, and hosts
a wide variety of exhibitions
and artistic, academic and
recreational events. ⊕ p. 55

MACBA →**1.4**B1

→ **1.4** B1
CCCB
Montalegre, 5
T 93 306 41 00
www.cccb.org
The Centre de Cultura
Contemporània de
Barcelona is an innovative
and versatile facility, focusing on the urban environ-
ment. Its programme of
events ranges from con-
temporary thought to new
manifestations of youth
culture, such as Sónar.

CCCB →**1.4**B1

→ **1.4** B2
BIBLIOTECA
DE CATALUNYA
Hospital, 56
T 93 270 23 00
www.bnc.cat
Founded at the beginning of
the 20th century and housed
in the imposing Gothic building of the old Hospital de
la Santa Creu since 1940.
The Biblioteca de Catalunya
contains over three million
documents and in 1998
underwent a major extension
during which new buildings
were added.

Biblioteca de Catalunya →**1.4**B2

→ **1.4** A3
SANT PAU DEL CAMP
Sant Pau, 101-103
The earliest records of this
Romanesque monastery
date from the 10th century.
The church, cloister,
chapterhouse and abbot's
residence were built
between the 12th and 14th
centuries, and painstakingly
restored in the 20th century.

Sant Pau del Camp →**1.4**A3

Art gallery →1.4 B1

Rambla del Raval →1.4 B2-3

Antic Hospital de la Santa Creu →1.4 B2

baroque architecture. It was originally a poor hospital and today its different rooms are home to the library, the Biblioteca Nacional de Catalunya, the Escola Massana, and the Institut d'Estudis Catalans.

TEATRE LLANTIOL
Riereta, 7 →1.4 A2
T 93 310 50 94
www.llantiol.com
Charming café-theatre with old-fashioned décor and unmistakeable character.

London Bar →1.4 B3

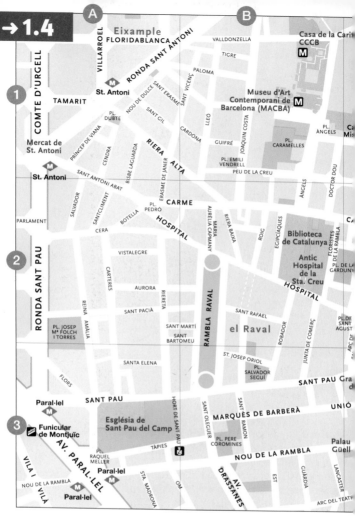

CASA PARRAMON
Carme, 8 →**1.4** C2
Luthiers since 1897.
Stringed instruments,
accessories and repairs.

MONS
Sant Pau, 6 →**1.4** C3
Jeweller's selling hand-
crafted pieces made from
fine materials.

FUTBOLMANIA
Ronda Sant Pau, 25 →**1.4** A2
Merchandising from all
the Spanish and European
squads.

LA CENTRAL DEL RAVAL
Elisabets, 6 →**1.4** C1
Bookshop housed in a
former church.
Pleasant café.

SASTRERIA
EL TRANSWAAL
Hospital, 67 →**1.4** B2
Since 1888. Hand-made
clothes and work uniforms.

THE AIR SHOP
Àngels, 20 →**1.4** B1
Inflatable artistic and
decorative elements of all
shapes and sizes.

And also
MERCAT DE
COLECCIONISTES
DE SANT ANTONI
Comte d'Urgell, 1 →**1.4** A1
Every Sunday, the
modernista Sant Antoni
Market hosts a collecto
fair selling second-han
books, comics, films...

ANTIC HOSPITAL
DE LA SANTA CREU
Hospital, 56 →**1.4** B2
Founded in 1401, it is a sup
example of civic Gothic and

11

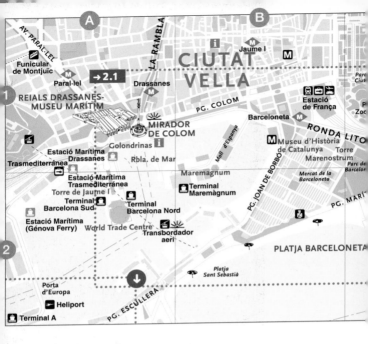

A city open to the sea

Seafront

Barcelona is a city open to the sea. The urban renewal undertaken before the 1992 Olympic Games reclaimed the entire seafront, dividing it into three stretches. The first, at the southern end, belongs to the port with its large area for goods vessels and the ferry terminals used by cruise passengers and the lines connecting Barcelona with the Balearic Islands and other Mediterranean ports. This stretch also includes Barceloneta

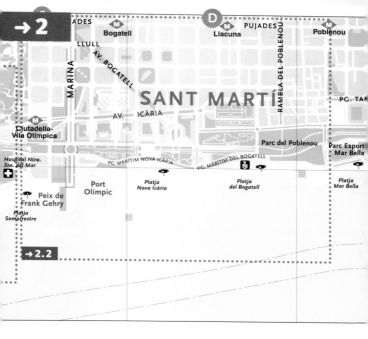

beach, a bathing area with a wide choice of dining options. The second area, the Olympic Village, has a well-equipped marina and another long beach which extends as far as the Forum zone, the third and final stretch of the seafront.

Don't miss

→ 2 A1 COLUMBUS MONUMENT

Plaça del Portal de la Pau | T 93 302 52 24 | barcelonaturisme.cat

The statue of Christopher Columbus presides over Barcelona harbour from the top of his column, 50 metres above the ground. At the same time, he encapsulates the city's seafaring tradition and the debt of gratitude it owes the sea, which witnessed the arrival of some of its founders and saw some of its explorers depart in search of new lands. A viewing gallery at the top of the tower boasts spectacular views of this meeting point.

→ 2 A1 REIALS DRASSANES - MUSEU MARÍTIM

Av. de les Drassanes, s/n | T 93 342 99 20 | www.mmb.cat

Barcelona's medieval shipyards (Reials Drassanes), which date from the 14th century, are worth visiting for two reasons. The first is the building, comprising a series of stone naves which are one of the finest and best-preserved examples of civic Gothic architecture. The second is the Museu Marítim, which brings together a wonderful collection of nautical equipment and ships. These include a replica of the galley used by Juan of Austria. ➕ p.56

Port Vell + Barceloneta

Barcelona's old harbour, the Port Vell, has berths for pleasure cruisers and yachts, areas with shops, offices and leisure amenities, services for boats, and quays used by the fishing fleet. Barceloneta was built in the mid-18th century between the harbour and the beach and consists of rectangular blocks. You can still feel the Mediterranean atmosphere you would expect to find in a fishing community.

Maremagnum
→ **2.1** B2
www.maremagnum.es
A retail and leisure centre wich enjoys a prime waterfront location and opens seven days a week including Sunday and public holidays, except for 25th December and 1st January. It has fashion boutiques and shoe shops; accessories and jewellery; cafés, ice-cream parlours and chocolate shops; toys; decoration, souvenirs, perfumery, hairdressers', photography and computer shops; nightclubs, bars and entertainment venues; and gastronomy. Opening times: 10am-10pm; restaurants, until 1am; bars and nightclubs, 11pm-4.30am; terraces, 1pm-4.30am.

ELX RESTAURANT
Moll d'Espanya, s/n, local 9
T 93 225 81 17
PÒSIT MARÍTIM
Moll d'Espanya, s/n
T 93 221 62 56
TAPAS BAR
Moll d'Espanya, s/n, local 10
T 93 225 81 80

Barcelona Bici
Bicycle hire by the hour or the day.
www.barcelonaturisme.cat

Barcelona Walking Tours Marina
Guided tours of the seafront (from April to October). Includes a pleasure cruise on one of the typical Golondrinas. Fridays and Saturdays at 10am in English; Saturdays at 10am in Spanish. Adults, 16,50 €; children, 6,50 €. Departure point: Columbus Monument.

Restaurants
The area is known for its typical restaurants serving a wide variety of rice dishes, fish and seafood.

More than 60 € → P. 88
LLUÇANÈS *
TORRE D'ALTA MAR

* Michelin-starred

DE MERCAT
Pl. de la Font, s/n → **2.1** C2
T 93 221 54 58
(20-30 €) + SET LUNCH MENU
Mediterranean cuisine in Barceloneta Market.
SAL CAFÉ
Passeig Marítim de la Barceloneta, 23 → **2.1** D2
T 93 224 07 07
(20-30 €) + SET LUNCH MENU
Modern beachfront restaurant. Contemporary fusion dishes.
7 PORTES
Passeig Isabel II, 14 → **2.1** C1

T 93 319 30 33
(30-50 €)
A BCN legend which has been serving paellas and other typical dishes since 1836. Open continuously, 1pm-1am.
Palau de Mar Area:
→ **2.1** C1
This former harbour warehouse dates from the 19th century and was renovated in 1992. It features restaurants specialising in seafood cuisine and rice dishes.
(30-50 €)
CAL PINXO
Plaça Pau Vila, s/n
T 93 221 22 11
LA GAVINA
Plaça Pau Vila, 1
T 93 221 05 95
MAGATZEM DEL PORT
Pl. Pau Vila, s/n
T 93 221 06 31
MERENDERO DE LA MARI
Plaça Pau Vila, 1
T 93 221 31 41
Barceloneta Area:
→ **2.1** C2-3 B3 → **2.2** A2
(30-60 €)
The city's classic seafood restaurants, some of them with a culinary tradition dating back more than 100 years. A treat for the palate.
CA LA NURI PLATJA
Passeig Marítim, 55
T 93 221 37 75
CAN COSTA
Passeig Joan de Borbó, 70
T 93 221 59 03

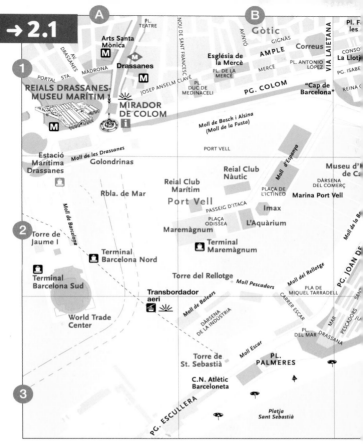

CAN MAJÓ
Almirall Aixada, 23
T 93 221 54 55

CAN RAMONET
Maquinista, 17
T 93 319 30 64

CAN SOLÉ
Sant Carles, 4
T 93 221 50 12

CHERIFF
Ginebra, 15
T 93 319 69 84

EL LOBITO
Ginebra, 9
T 93 319 91 64

L'ARRÒS
Passeig Joan de Borbó, 12
T 93 221 26 46

SUQUET DE L'ALMIRALL
Passeig Joan de Borbó, 65
T 93 221 62 33

Cafés and bars

EL VASO DE ORO
Balboa, 7 →2.1 C2
Historic beer house. Small
bar serving excellent tapas.

JAI·CA
Ginebra, 13 →2.1 C2
T 93 310 50 94
Another classic. Typical,
tasty tapas.

LA BOMBETA
Pl. de la Maquinista, 3
→2.1 C2
Tapas bar which is a
neighbourhood classic.
Delicious, spicy *bombes*
(mince and potato balls
in breadcrumbs with hot
sauce in the centre).

**MUSEU D'HISTÒRIA
DE CATALUNYA TERRACE**
Pl. de Pau Vila, 3 →2.1 C1

Bar and café with splendid
panoramic views of the
harbour.

Shops

BODEGA FERMÍN
Sant Carles, 16 →2.1 C2
Specialises in wines and
vermouths sold from the
barrel. A wide variety of
wines and cavas.

EL REMITGER
Passeig Joan de Borbó, 63
→2.1 C3
Sells nautical clothing
and fishing tackle.

FORN BALUARD
Baluard, 38-40 →2.1 C2
An artisan baker's
producing bread that
tastes like it did in the
old days.

Seafront

Sant Martí
Vila Olímpica

The district of Sant Martí, which stretches from the Parc de la Ciutadella and Plaça de les Glòries to the Besòs River, is immersed in a complete process of renewal, which includes the extension of the Diagonal as far as the sea and the establishment of the technology district 22@. The Olympic Village, built near the seafront to house the athletes for the 1992 Games, was the cornerstone of this transformation.

Barcelona Mar

Two-hour yacht trips along the Barcelona coastline. Enjoy panoramic views of the city from the sea as you sip a glass of cava. Includes admission to the **Museu Marítim** and the historic schooner, the **Pailebot Santa Eulàlia**. April to October. Times: Wednesday at 5pm; Sunday at 11.30am and 2pm. Adults, 30 €; children, 16 €. Departure point: Centre Municipal de Vela-CMV. Moll de Gregal, s/n - Port Olímpic.

Restaurants

More than 60 € → P. 88
ENOTECA *

AGUA
Passeig Marítim de la Barceloneta, 30 →**2.2** A2
T 93 225 12 72
(30-40 €)
Mediterranean cuisine right on the beach. Good value for money.

BESTIAL
Ramon Trias Fargas, 2-4
→**2.2** A2
T 93 224 04 07
(30-50 €) + SET LUNCH MENU
Terrace and garden right on the beach.

Mediterranean cuisine with an Italian twist.

ELS PESCADORS
Plaça Prim, 1 →**2.2** D2
T 93 225 20 18
(+ than 50 €)
Rafa Medrán and his team create freshly made dishes based on traditional and seafood recipes.

ELS «POLLOS» DE LLULL
Ramon Turró, 13 →**2.2** A1
T 93 221 32 06
(10-20 €) + GROUP MENU
Specialists in spit-roast chickens. Inexpensive.

LA FONDA
DEL PORT OLÍMPIC
Moll de Gregal, 7 →**2.2** B3
T 93 221 22 10
(30-50 €) + SET LUNCH MENU
Extensive à la carte menu. Mediterranean cuisine.

XIRINGUITO ESCRIBÀ
Av. Litoral, 42 →**2.2** B2
T 93 221 07 29
(30-50 €)
Sea views combined with seafood cuisine. Make sure you try the desserts.

Cafés and bars

EL TIO CHE
Rambla del Poblenou, 44
→**2.2** D1
Since 1912. Serves home-made orxata, a milky drink made from tiger nuts, and granitas.

REMBRANDT
Marina, 20 →**2.2** A2

A café in the morning and cocktail bar at night.

Shops

AL PUNT DE TROBADA
Badajoz, 24 →**2.2** C1
T 93 225 05 85
Bicycle hire, seven days a week.

ICÀRIA SPORTS
Av. d'Icària, 180 →**2.2** A2
T 93 221 17 78
Shop specialising in in-line skates. They are also available for hire.

ÚLTIMA PARADA
Taulat, 93 →**2.2** D1
Interior design shop specialising in vintage furniture, particularly from the 1960s and 1970s.

And also

CASINO DE BARCELONA
Marina, 19-21 →**2.2** A2
www.casino-barcelona.com
A casino by the sea, with restaurants, bars and a discotheque.

CEMENTIRI
DEL POBLENOU
Taulat, 2 →**2.2** C2
Opened in 1775, this was the first cemetery in BCN to be built outside the city walls. It was destroyed by Napoleon's troops in 1813, and rebuilt in 1849 with its pantheons by renowned architects and modernista and noucentista sculptors.

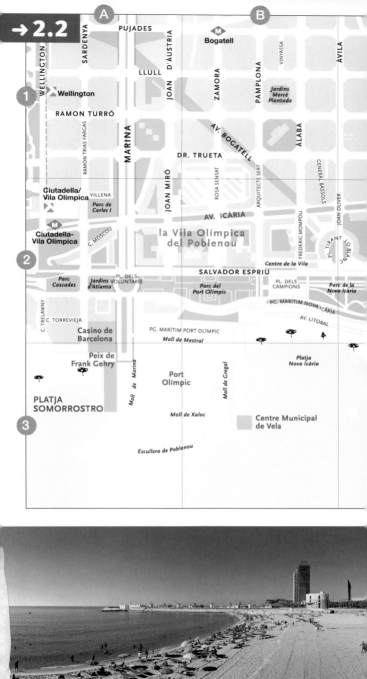

A   B

PUJADES

SARDENYA

WELLINGTON

Ⓜ Bogatell

JOAN D'ÀUSTRIA

LLULL

ZAMORA

PAMPLONA

VINYASSA

ÀVILA

1 ▲ **Wellington**

RAMON TURRÓ

Jardins Mercè Plantada

RAMON TRIAS FARGAS

MARINA

AV. BOGATELL

ÀLABA

DR. TRUETA

ROSA SENSAT

ARQUITECTE SERT

GENERAL BASSOLS

JOAN OLIVER

JOAN MIRÓ

AV. ICÀRIA

FREDERIC MOMPOU

PL. TIRANT LO BLANC

Ciutadella/ Vila Olímpica   VILLENA
Parc de Carles I

C. MOSCOU

la Vila Olímpica del Poblenou

Centre de la Vila

Ⓜ Ciutadella- Vila Olímpica

2

SALVADOR ESPRIU

Parc Cascades

Jardins d'Atlanta   PL. DELS VOLUNTARIS

Parc del Port Olímpic

PL. DELS CAMPIONS

Parc de la Nova Icària

PG. MARÍTIM NOVA ICÀRIA

C. TRELAWNY   C. TORREVIEJA

AV. LITORAL

PG. MARÍTIM PORT OLÍMPIC

Casino de Barcelona

Moll de Mestral

Platja Nova Icària

Peix de Frank Gehry

Moll de Marina

Port Olímpic

Moll de Gregal

PLATJA SOMORROSTRO

Moll de Xaloc

Centre Municipal de Vela

3

Escullera de Poblenou

17 **Nova Icària beach →2.2** B2

Sant Martí
Fòrum

The city's hosting of the Forum of Cultures in 2004 led to a series of building developments that transformed the seafront of Sant Martí and completed the renewal of Barcelona's coastline. Following innovative guidelines, the city built a new congress complex (CCIB) on the Forum site, which can host up to 15,000 people, and placed it over a vast water-regulation and treatment facility, heralding a space for a sustainable future.

Forum Precinct

One of the latest urban-planning interventions based on the Barcelona "model" (which involves taking advantage of an event in order to improve services and infrastructures). Covering an area of 320,000 m², the precinct is one of the biggest cultural and recreational public spaces on the planet. In addition to the Forum Building, the Barcelona International Convention Centre and the Photovoltaic pergola, the site also has a marina with 170 mooring berths for boats measuring between 10 and 25 m in length, and 31 berths for large yachts up to 80 m in length. It also has an innovative bathing area and vast plaza (over 100,000 m²) which hosts a wide range of events including the Primavera Sound Festival and the April Flamenco Fair.

Museums

MUSEU DE CIÈNCIES NATURALS

Rbla. Prim, 2 →**2.3** C2
www.museuciencies.bcn.cat
Housed in the Forum Building, it hosts the exhibition *Planet Life* about zoology, geology and botany.

Restaurants

EL COMEDOR

P. Garcia Faria, 37-47 →**2.3** A2
T 93 531 60 40
(30-50 €) + GROUP MENU
Mediterranean cuisine, right on the seafront, with flavours of home-cooking.

ELS PEIXATERS DE LA MEDITERRÀNIA

Passeig de Garcia Fària, 33
→**2.3** A2
T 93 266 38 84
(30-40 €) + SET LUNCH MENU
Specialises in locally caught fresh fish and seafood.

ESCOLA D'HOSTALERIA

Passeig del Taulat, 243
→**2.3** A2
T 93 453 29 04
(20-40 €) + SET LUNCH MENU
Find out what the great chefs of the future are cooking in Barcelona.

INDIGO

Pg. Taulat, 262-264 →**2.3** B2
T 93 507 07 07
(30-50 €)
International cuisine with fabulous sea views.

LA CANTINA

Pellaires, 30-38 →**2.3** A2
T 93 307 09 74
(20-40 €) + SET LUNCH MENU
Traditional and fusion cuisine in an old factory.

LA OCA MAR

Platja de la Nova Mar Bella
→**2.3** A2
T 93 225 01 00
(20-40 €) + SET LUNCH MENU
Simulates a boat floating on the sea. Contemporary cuisine.

SAGARDI EUSKAL TABERNA

Av. Diagonal, 3 →**2.3** C1
T 93 356 04 76
(20-40 €)
Basque cuisine with an endless variety of canapés and grilled meat and fish.

Cafés and bars

In the cutting-edge, seafront hotels: **Pistaccio Lobby Bar** and **Brisa Pool Bar** (Pg. Taulat, 262); **The Corner Bar** and **The Gym Bar** (Av. Diagonal, 1). At the Diagonal Mar shopping centre: tapas and beers (**Barcelonia, Tapas Bar, Kurz & Gut**); coffee and ice creams (**Cal Tuset, Jamaica, Kokoa, Häagen-Dazs**); fruit juices (**Passion Fruits**).

Shops

Shopping centre:
DIAGONAL MAR
→ P. 87

And also

PARK & RIDE

Av. Eduard Maristany, s/n
→**2.3** D1
Parking spaces for mobile homes. 25 € per day. Maximum stay: 72 h.

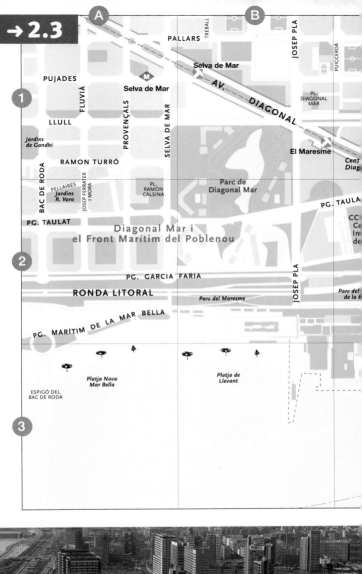

A   B

TREBALL

PALLARS

JOSEP PLA

PUIGCERDÀ

Selva de Mar

AV.

DIAGONAL

PUJADES

Selva de Mar

FLUVIÀ

PROVENÇALS

SELVA DE MAR

PL. DIAGONAL MAR

1

LLULL

Jardins de Gandhi

RAMON TURRÓ

El Maresme

Cent Diag

BAC DE RODA

PELLAIRES
Jardins R. Varo

JOSEP FERRATER I MORA

PL. RAMÓN CALSINA

Parc de
Diagonal Mar

PG. TAULA

PG. TAULAT

CC
Ce
In
de

Diagonal Mar i
el Front Marítim del Poblenou

2

PG. GARCIA FARIA

JOSEP PLA

RONDA LITORAL

Parc del Maresme

Parc del
de la l

PG. MARÍTIM DE LA MAR BELLA

ESPIGÓ DEL
BAC DE RODA

Platja Nova
Mar Bella

Platja de
Llevant

3

19 **Forum Precinct →2.3** C2

L'Eixample
+ Gràcia

The Eixample-Gràcia is Barcelona's central area. With its rational grid layout, designed by Ildefons Cerdà, which abounds in *modernista* gems, the leafy, light-filled Eixample defines Barcelona's personality: an enterprising city known for its culture and commerce, which set its sights on the future in the 19th century and is now one of the world's major cities. Gràcia, with its narrow streets and timeless charm, epitomises the old rural villages which were annexed by Barcelona without losing any of their character. Visitors will find almost everything they need in this central area of the city, which has retained its human scale, making it the perfect place to have a relaxing stroll and where there is a surprise around every corner.

Don't miss

→ 3 C3 BASILICA OF THE SAGRADA FAMÍLIA 🏛

Mallorca, 401 | T 93 207 30 31 | www.sagradafamilia.cat

Gaudí devoted the last 40 years of his life to this immense, cathedral-like building. It is characterised by its eight tapering towers, surmounted by vividly coloured ceramic pinnacles. Each tower is 100 metres high but will be dwarfed by the future dome, which will stand 170 metres when completed. The church, which was begun in 1882 and is scheduled for completion in 2025, is one of Barcelona's most visited landmarks. ➕ p. 60

→ 3 B3 LA PEDRERA (CASA MILÀ) 🏛

Provença, 261-265 | T 902 400 973 | www.fundaciocaixacatalunya.org

La Casa Milà – dubbed by locals as La Pedrera, Catalan for stone quarry – has an outstanding undulating façade which evokes incredible stone waves. Originally designed as a residential block, today part of the building is a cultural centre. The Espai Gaudí, in the attic space, traces the architect's research and secrets. The restored flats display the wide range of plaster mouldings, carpentry and ironwork. But the main surprise awaits on the roof: a forest of sculptural chimneys. ➕ p. 62

→ 3 C1 PARK GÜELL 🏛

Olot, s/n | T 93 413 24 00

This garden-city conceals some of the finest examples of Gaudí's fantastic imagination. It is reached via a staircase presided over by a large ceramic dragon. Above it, are the columns of the hypostyle chamber which underpins the plaza with its magnificent views of Barcelona, with a curving bench around its perimeter covered in fragments of tiles, crockery and bottles. These works are surrounded by arcades, houses and boundary paths. ➕ p. 64

Quadrat d'Or
+ Gaudí Trail [1]

The Quadrat d'Or – Golden Square – is the heritage district that brings together a dazzling array of *modernista* architecture, built in the centre of Barcelona in the early years of the 20th century. Gaudí, Domènech i Montaner, Puig i Cadafalch and other great *modernista* architects left their legacy here in the shape of innovative buildings which still retain their original splendour.

Barcelona Walking Tours
Modernisme
Two-hour walking tour led by professional guides exploring the Quadrat d'Or, the centre of *modernista* Barcelona: a true open-air museum. Landmarks include works by Gaudí (Casa Milà, Casa Batlló), Domènech i Montaner (Palau de la Música Catalana, Casa Lleó Morera, Fundació Tàpies) and Puig i Cadafalch (Casa Amatller, Casa Terrades).
Price: adults, 13 €; children, 5 €.
Times: Friday and Saturday, 4pm (English); Saturday, 4pm (Catalan and Spanish).
Departs from the Turisme de Barcelona Information Office (Pl. de Catalunya, 17-s).

Gaudí Trail
Includes tours of three major landmarks by this architectural genius, all of them World Heritage Sites. They are icons of art rather than buildings and they are all open to visitors. They include Casa Batlló (Passeig de Gràcia, 43; www.casabatllo.es), the Casa Milà "La Pedrera" (Passeig de Gràcia, 92;

www.fundaciocaixacatalunya.org) and Sagrada Família (Mallorca, 401; www.sagradafamilia.cat). Download the audioguide *Gaudí's Barcelona* onto your MP3 player (http://bcnshop.barcelonaturisme.com).

Art galleries
The rectangle of streets Diputació, Aragó, Enric Granados and Pg. de Gràcia is home to the largest number of galleries in Barcelona.
For information www.artbarcelona.es

Museums
MUSEU EGIPCI
FUND. ARQUEOLÒGICA CLOS
València, 284 →3.1 B2
www.museuegipci.com
Thematic collection of Egyptian antiquities. More than 1,000 major exhibits.
FUNDACIÓ FRANCISCO GODIA
Diputació, 250 →3.1 A2
www.fundacionfgodia.org
Medieval art, ceramics and modern painting collection.
FUNDACIÓ JOAN BROSSA
Provença, 318 →3.1 B1
www.fundaciojoanbrossa.cat
Object poems, visual poems, installations, artist's books, posters and

films by Joan Brossa.
MUSEU DEL MODERNISME CATALÀ
Balmes, 48 →3.1 A2
www.mmcat.cat
Modernista objects, paintings and sculptures.

Restaurants

More than 60 € → P. 88
CAELIS **
CINC SENTITS *
DROLMA *
FONDA GAIG
GAIG *
GALAXÓ
LASARTE **
MANAIRÓ *
MOMENTS *
MONVÍNIC
MOO *

* Michelin-starred

CASA CALVET
Casp, 48 →3.1 B3
T 93 412 40 12
(+50 €) + SET LUNCH MENU
In a house by Gaudí, exquisite Catalan cuisine.
GRESCA
Provença, 230 →3.1 A1
T 93 451 61 93
(40-50 €) + SET LUNCH MENU
Catalan cuisine by the chef Rafael Peña.
LOIDI
Mallorca, 248 →3.1 B1
T 93 492 92 92
(40-50 €) + TASTING MENU
Traditional Basque cuisine reinvented with the flavour

of Martín Berasategui.

PETIT COMITÈ
Passatge de la Concepció,
13 →**3.1** A1
T 93 550 06 20
(30-50 €) + SET LUNCH MENU
The chef Fermí Puig returns
to his Catalan roots.

TAPAÇ 24
Diputació, 269 →**3.1** B2
T 93 488 09 77
(20-30 €)
Tasting dishes and tapas
by the El Bulli-trained chef
Carles Abellán.

Cafés and bars

BAR VELÓDROMO
Muntaner, 213 →**3.1**A1
A time-honoured classic

(opens from 6am-3am)
promoted by the Moritz
brewery and with the chef
Carles Abellán at the helm.

CASA ALFONSO
Roger de Llúria, 6 →**3.1** B3
Since 1934. Landmark
tapas and sandwich bar.
Excellent delicatessen.

DRY MARTINI
Aribau, 162 →**3.1** A1
Classic cocktail bar with
vintage bottles displayed
on its shelves and an art
collection on its walls.

MAURI
Rambla de Catalunya, 102
→**3.1** A1
Excellent cake shop with a
popular tea room.

Shops

You'll find some of
Barcelona's leading fash-
ion outlets on the Pg. de
Gràcia and surrounding
streets: Furest, Miró,
Armand Basi, Loewe,
Camper, Mango…

Shopping centres:
BULEVARD ROSA
EL CORTE INGLÉS
EL TRIANGLE
→ P. 87

BAGUÉS-MASRIERA
Pg. de Gràcia, 41 →**1.3** B2
Founded in 1839. Exclusiv
art-nouveau and art-deco
jewellery.

Gràcia
+ Gaudí Trail (2)

The imprint of *modernista* architecture, particularly Gaudí's, can also be found in Gràcia and, to the north, in the lower foothills of the Collserola Ridge: from the Casa Vicens to the magnificent Park Güell. These are all contained in a neighbourhood with a strongly defined personality set around squares that reflect its vitality and close-knit community.

Gaudí Trail
The old village of Gràcia, which was separate from Barcelona until 1897, is home to two major Gaudí landmarks: the **Casa Vicens**, his first major work, and the **Park Güell**, considered by many to be his greatest masterpiece. The park contains two interesting cultural facilities: the **Centre d'Interpretació del Park Güell** (MUHBA) and the **Casa Museu Gaudí**, his former home which contains a major collection of objects associated with or designed by Gaudí. Download the audioguide *Gaudí's Barcelona* (http://bcnshop.barcelonaturisme.com).

Museums
FUNDACIÓ
FOTO COLECTÀNIA
Julián Romea, 6 →3 A2
www.colectania.es
Brings together over 2,000 photos by Spanish and Portuguese photographers from 1950. Temporary exhibitions.

Restaurants

More than 60 € → P. 88
ALKÍMIA *
ROIG ROBÍ

* Michelin-starred

BILBAO
Perill, 33 →**3.2** A3
T 93 458 96 24
(30-50 €) + SET LUNCH MENU
Traditional Basque cuisine with a Catalan twist.

BOTAFUMEIRO
Gran de Gràcia, 81 →**3.2** A2
T 93 218 42 30
(+50 €) + GROUP MENU
The doyen of BCN's seafood restaurants. Galician cuisine.

D.O.
Verdi, 36 →**3.2** B2
T 93 218 96 73
(25-35 €) DINNER ONLY
Wines and creative tapas until 1am, in a contemporary setting.

EL JARDÍ DE L'ÀPAT
Albert Llanas, 2 →**3.2** C1
T 93 285 77 50
(20-30 €) + SET LUNCH MENU
A villa with a garden, terrace and beautiful views. Chargrilled meat and vegetables.

ENVALIRA
Plaça del Sol, 13 →**3.2** A2
T 93 218 58 13
(30-40 €)
A Gràcia classic. Market-fresh cuisine, rice and seafood dishes.

LA LLAVOR
DELS ORÍGENS
Ramón y Cajal, 12 →**3.2** A2
T 93 213 60 31
(20-30 €) + SET LUNCH MENU
Catalan cuisine from 12.30am to 1am.

VERDI 82
Verdi, 82 →**3.2** B2
T 93 415 01 01
(15-25 €)
Menu featuring market-fresh traditional Catalan cuisine. Open for dinner only.

Cafés and bars
CAFÈ DEL SOL
Plaça del Sol, 16 →**3.2** A2
A neighbourhood classic. The place for a pre-lunch drink and snack on the terrace beneath the magnolia trees.

BODEGA MANOLO
Torrent de les Flors, 101
→**3.2** B2
Genuine neighbourhood bodega with a unique atmosphere.

NOISE I ART
Topazi, 26
→**3.2** A2
Modern, laid-back atmosphere. A chic lounge bar.

ROURE
Luís Antúnez, 7 →**3.2** A3
Since 1889. 7am-1am
Breakfast, aperitifs, tapas, lunch, dinner and drinks.

SALAMBÓ
Torrijos, 51 →**3.2** B2
Two levels: pool room and lounge bar. Drinks bar and restaurant.

Shops
AMARANTO
Sant Domènec, 23 →**3.2** A3
Jewellery by young

el Putxet i Farró
ESCIPIÓ
BALLESTER
Casa Tosquella
PÀDUA
PL. VENTURA GASSOL
PL. ST. JOAQUIM
RONDA GENERAL MITRE
HOMER
REP. ARGENTINA
AV. VALLCARCA
MARE DE DÉU DEL COLL
VERDI
PARK GÜELL
MUHBA Pa
Casa del Gu
LARRARD
la Salut

Església dels Josepets
PL. LESSEPS
Santuari
Sant Josep de
la Muntanya
Mercat de
Lesseps
Jardins
Menéndez
y Pelayo
Clu

Lesseps
PL. MANÉ I FLAQUER
PL. TORRE
GRAN DE GRÀCIA
TRAV. DE DALT

AV. PRINCEP D'ASTÚRIES
CAROLINES
Casa Vicens
PL. TRILLA
Fontana
RBLA. PRAT
MATEU
ASTÚRIES
TRAV. SANT ANTONI
PL. ANNA FRANK
MONTSENY
TORRENT DE L'OLLA
Jardins
Mestre
Balcells
ST. SALVADOR
PL. NORD
MARTÍ
BIADA
PROVIDÈNCIA
Vila de Gràcia
ROBÍ
PL. SANTA CREU
VIRREINA
OR
PL. DIAMANT
PERLA
VERDI
FLORS
PL. ROVIRA I TRIAS
DE
LEGALITAT
JOAN BLANQUES
TORRENT
ENCARNACIÓ
ST. LLUÍS
ESCORIAL
ALEGRE DE DAIT
CAMÈ

Gràcia
Mercat de
la Llibertat
PL. LLIBERTAT
PERE SERAFÍ
ROS DE OLANO
PL. SOL
PL. REVOLUCIÓ SETEMBRE 1868
TORRIJOS
TORRENT D'EN VIDALET
Joanic
PL. JOANIC

PL. GAL·LA PLACÍDIA
GRAN DE GRÀCIA
TRAV. DE GRÀCIA
RAMÓN Y CAJAL
el Camp

LUIS ANTÚNEZ
RIERA DE ST. MIQUEL
PLC. ST. MIQUEL
PL. NARCÍS OLLER
MINERVA
Pl. Vila
de Gràcia
GOYA
Jardins
Salvador
Espriu
BONAVISTA
Casa Fuster
Cambra de Comerç
PL. REI
Casa Serra JOAN CARLES I
Palau
Robert
Fundació Suñol
Palau Baro de Quadras
Diagonal
TORRENT DE L'OLLA
PERILL
Mercat de
l'Abaceria Central
PL. POBLE ROMANÍ
PL. RASPALL
PL. DE GATO PÉREZ
LLIBERTAT
CAMPRODON
MILÀ I
FONTANALS
BAILÈN
GIRONA
CÒRSEGA
PL. JOHN LENNON
PG. DE SANT JOAN
ROGER DE FLOR
NÀPOLS
Grasso
Gràcia N
ST. A
Casa Terrades "Les Punxes"
ROSSELL

---

designers (shop and showroom).

BOO
La Perla, 20 →**3.2** B2
Fashion and accessories by American, English and Swedish designers.

CAMISERIA PONS
Gran de Gràcia, 49 →**3.2** A3
Century-old shop selling contemporary fashions.

L'HORA EXACTA
Gran de Gràcia, 42 →**3.2** A3
Time-honoured watch and clockmakers. Cubist-,

modernista- and medieval-inspired designs.

MENCHÉN TOMÀS
Riera de Sant Miquel, 37 →**3.2** A3
Smart clothes for women and urban design.

LYDIA DELGADO
Minerva, 21 →**3.2** A3
One of Barcelona's great fashion designers for women.

SUITE
Verdi, 6 →**3.2** B2
Fashion by BCN's trend-setting young designers.

SULA SHOP
Or, 42 →**3.2** B2
Hand-crafted textiles, basketry and decorative items.

VIALIS
Verdi, 39 →**3.2** B2
Unmistakeable, comfortable designer shoes made from the finest materials.

And also

CINEMES VERDI
Verdi, 32 →**3.2** A3
BCN's leading arthouse

Sants
+ Montjuïc

Sants-Montjuïc is Barcelona's largest district, covering a surface area equivalent to a fifth of the municipal territory. It comprises neighbourhoods with their own distinct personalities, such as the former villages of Sants, Hostafrancs, Poble-sec and La Bordeta, as well as the harbour and its free-trade area, the Zona Franca. They are located in the environs of Montjuïc Hill, surmounted by the castle that used to guard its coastline. This "green lung", which was built on for the 1929 Exhibition and the 1992 Olympics, is home to the Olympic Ring, major museums, the Botanical Gardens and other facilities for the entire community.

Don't miss

→ 4 B3 MUSEU NACIONAL D'ART DE CATALUNYA (MNAC)

Parc de Montjuïc, s/n | T 93 622 03 76 | www.mnac.cat

The Museu Nacional d'Art de Catalunya brings together the most important collections of Catalan art. Housed in the Palau Nacional, an iconic landmark which stands out against the Barcelona skyline, the museum showcases a 1,000 years of local creativity. Its collection of Romanesque art from the Pyrenees is unique. It also has noteworthy Gothic collections and a selection of art spanning the late 19th to the mid-20th centuries. ➕ p.70

→ 4 C3 FUNDACIÓ JOAN MIRÓ

Parc de Montjuïc, s/n | T 93 443 94 70 | www.fundaciomiro-bcn.org

Joan Miró, the world-renowned Barcelona-born artist and one of the leading figures of the surrealist movement, bequeathed this foundation and study centre to his home town. It was designed by Josep Lluís Sert and exhibits a large selection of Miró's works, organises exhibitions by other major artists and fosters creativity by young artists. The Fundació Miró boasts magnificent views of the city and is surrounded by trees and sculptures. ➕ p.71

→ 4 B3 FONT MÀGICA

Pl. de Carles Buïgas, 1 | T 93 310 50 94

Water, light and colour. The engineer Carles Buïgas harnessed these three elements to design his Magic Fountain at the foot of Montjuïc Hill. It consists of three concentric circles of water jets which create a water sculpture of constantly changing, flowing forms: a poetic spectacle set to music, which Barcelona uses for its great city festivals and celebrations.

A

SANTS

BRASIL

B

LES COR

Badal

Pl. del
Centre

1

BADAL

Mercat
de Sants

Sa
Est

Estació d'Autobusos
Sants

Estació
de Sants

AVE

Sta. Eulàlia

Mercat
Nou

Pl. de Sants

Parc Espanya
Industrial

SANTS

Pavelló de
l'Espanya
Industrial

TARRAGONA

BADAL

Hostafrancs

Mercat
d'Hostafrancs

Tarragona

2

PL.
ILDEFONS
CERDÀ

Fira de
Barcelona-
Gran Via

Gran Via

SANTS-

GRAN VIA CORTS CATALANES

Magòria-
La Campana

Espanya

PL.
ESP

Espa

PG. ZONA FRANCA

MONTJUÏC

CaixaForum

Poble Espanyol de Barcelona

Fundació Fran Daurel

Palau de

Pavelló Mies van der Rohe

FONT MÀGIC.
DE MONTJUÏC

Mercat
de la Marina

→4.2

MUSEU NACIONAL D'ART
DE CATALUNYA (MNAC)
INEFC

Ciuta
del Teatr

3

Torre de
Calatrava

Piscines Bernat Picornell

Museu
Etnològic

Grup
Can Clos

Anella Olímpica

Jardins
Joan Maragall

Palauet
Albéniz

Jardins
Font de

Fossar de
la Pedrera

Palau Sant Jordi

Sot del
Migdia

→4.3

Museu Olímpic
i de l'Esport

Estadi Olímpic
Lluís Companys

Parc de Montjuïc

Jardí Botànic

Jardí de
Petra Kelly

Jardí Botànic
de Barcelona

Cementiri de
Montjuïc

4

Mirador
del Migdia

Castell de
Montjuïc

Camí de Ronda

Far

RONDA LIT

Plaça Espanya + Trade fair site

The Plaça d'Espanya is one of Barcelona's main traffic hubs. It connects the roads from the southern coast with the city's main arteries, including the Gran Via, Paral·lel and Carrer Tarragona. It is also the gateway to Montjuïc and the trade fair site, Fira de Barcelona, with its halls set out at the foot of the hill.

Poble Espanyol de Barcelona

This special precinct was built for the 1929 International Exhibition. Designed like a village, with its own main square, it is an open-air museum showcasing all the Spanish architectural styles through replicas of famous landmark buildings. It is currently one of the city's most popular leisure attractions and is home to all kinds of craft workshops, shops, entertainment companies, art foundations, performing-arts and fine-art schools, restaurants, bars and discotheques. It also hosts activities for the whole family, particularly children. Every night in summer it provides a superb setting for concerts and other entertainments. Opening times: Monday, 9am-8pm; Tuesday to Thursday, 9am-2am; Friday and Saturday, 9am-5am; Sunday, 9am-11pm. www.poble-espanyol.com

Museos

MUSEU DEL ROCK
Pl. d'Espanya →4.1 B2
www.museudelrock.com
The only museum of its kind in Europe. It has rooms devoted to The Beatles, The Rolling Stones and the virtual attraction On Stage.

Restaurants

More than 60 € → P. 88
EVO *
* Michelin-starred

EL BISTROT DE SANTS
Plaça Països Catalans, s/n →4 C1
T 93 503 53 00
(35-50 €)
Mediterranean cuisine in a cosy atmosphere.

LA CLARA
Gran Via, 442 →4.1 C2
T 93 289 34 60
(30-40 €) + GROUP MENU
Two levels. Downstairs, rustic tapas bar, 8am to midnight; upstairs, restaurant serving Catalan cuisine.

LOLITA TAPERÍA
Tamarit, 104 →4.1 C3
T 93 424 52 31
(20-30 €)
Offers a selection of the most popular Spanish tapas.

OLEUM
Parc de Montjuïc, s/n →4.1 B3
T 93 289 06 79

(25-50 €) + SET LUNCH MENU
Inside the MNAC. Creative Mediterranean cuisine.

RÍAS DE GALÍCIA
Lleida, 7 →4.1 C2
T 93 424 81 52
(+60 €) + GROUP MENU
The finest seafood and fish from the Galician coast.

TICKETS
Av. Paral·lel, 164 →4.1 C3
T 93 292 42 50
(40-45 €)
Excellent tapas and small servings of traditional dishes served up by the Adrià brothers.

Cafés and bars

The cultural attractions MNAC, CaixaForum, Poble Espanyol and the Ciutat del Teatre have excellent bars and cafeterias. You can also enjoy a drink or snack at the refreshment kiosks in front of the Magic Fountain.

Shops

Shopping centres:
ARENAS DE BARCELONA → Pág. 87

The Sants-Creu Coberta shopping area (→4.1 A1 B1) is considered Europe's longest retail thoroughfare and has 500 shops and two municipal markets.

Highlights

→ 4.1 B1
PARC DE JOAN MIRÓ
Laid out in the 1980s the park marked the beginning of Barcelona's new urban planning. It covers a surface area equivalent to four blocks in the Eixample and combines wooded and paved areas. It is overlooked by Miró's 22-metre-high sculpture *Woman and Bird*.

Parc de Joan Miró → **4.1** A2

→ 4.1 A3
PAVELLÓ
MIES VAN DER ROHE
Av. Marquès de Comillas, s/n
T 93 423 40 16
www.miesbcn.com
This modern masterpiece was designed by Van der Rohe as the German Pavilion for the 1929 International Exhibition. It was demolished after the event but faithfully rebuilt in 1986. It now houses an architectural foundation. 🔵 p. 72

Mies van der Rohe Pavilion → **4.1** A

→ 4.1 B2
CAIXAFORUM
Av. Marquès de Comillas, 6
T 93 476 86 00
www.obrasocial.lacaixa.es
Puig i Cadafalch created a paradigm of industrial art nouveau with this factory. The "la Caixa" Foundation restored the building, preserving its original features, and today it hosts art exhibitions, concerts, literary and film events... 🔵 p. 73

CaixaForum → **4.1** A2

→ 4.1 A3
POBLE ESPANYOL
Av. Marquès de Comillas, 13
T 93 508 63 00
www.poble-espanyol.com
The Poble Espanyol is a compendium of Spanish vernacular architecture. Its network of narrow streets brings together replicas of 117 buildings from different areas of Spain.

Poble Espanyol → **4.1** A2

Venetian Towers →4.1B2

Mercat de les Flors →4.1B3

And also

CIUTAT DEL TEATRE
Lleida, 59 →4.1B3
A complex entirely devoted
to the performing arts.
Located in a 19th-century-
style building from
the 1929 International
Exhibition, it includes
the **Mercat de les Flors**
(dance), the **Teatre Lliure**
(theatre) and the **Institut
del Teatre** (school), with
six theatre spaces seating
more than 2,000 people.
EL PARAL·LEL
A legendary avenue
dating from the early
20th century known
for its slightly risqué
popular entertainment
(Barcelona's Montmartre).
It is gradually regaining
its former splendour with
the restoration of its
historic music halls such
as **El Molino** (built in 1898
and refurbished in 2010),
and theatres, including
the **Victòria, Apolo, Condal**
and **Arteria Paral·lel**.

services, including a shuttle bus when necessary.
Montjuïc site
Eight halls at the foot of
Montjuïc, Barcelona's
trade-fair hill.
Gran Via site
Six halls in an expanding
area featuring contem-
porary interventions by
architects of the calibre of
Toyo Ito, Alejandro Zaera
and Arata Isozaki. Further
information on p. 55.
www.firabcn.cat

→ 4.1

Estació de Sants

Parc Espanya Industrial

Pavelló de l'Espanya Industrial

Hostafrancs

Tarragona

Hostafrancs

Mercat d'Hostafrancs

"DO I C

Parc Joan Mi

Centre Comerç Arenas de Bar

Museu d

Espanya

PL. ESPANYA

Espanya

Espanya

la Font de la Guatlla

FRUCTUÓS

FONT FLORIDA

Palau 8

Palau 1

Fira de Barcel Montju

CaixaForum (Casaramona)

Poble Espanyol de Barcelona

Palau de Congressos

Palau 2

Fundació Fran Daurel

Pavelló Mies van der Rohe

FONT MÀGICA DE MONTJUÏC

Palau 7

Camp de rugby de la Foixarda

Pista d'hípica de la Foixarda

Palau 6

Barcelona Teatre Musica

Parc de Montjuïc

AV. DE L'ESTADI

MUSEU NACIONAL D'ART DE CATALUNYA (MNAC)

INEFC

Piscines Bernat Picornell

Torre de Calatrava

Teatre de les

Ciutat del Teatre

Tea

→ 4.1+

Europa Fira

Parc de l'Alhambra

Jardins de Valentí Petit

AV. DE LA GRANVIA

L'HOSPITALET DE LLOBREGAT

Centre Comercial Gran Via 2

CIÈNCIES

Pavelló 2   Pavelló 3

ARQUITECTURA

Pavelló 1   Pavelló 4

Mercat de la Marina

Jardins de l'Arboreda

Pavelló 6

Pavelló 8

SANTS-MONTJUÏC

Jardins Ca l'Alena

Fira de Barcelona

The trade fair opened in 1932 in the pavilions used for the 1929 International Exhibition. It now has a second site nea the airport and is Spain's largest trade-fair site in terms of surface area (365,000 m² of exhibition space) and one of Europe's leading exhibition facilities. Both sites have state-of-the-art infrastructures and offer a wide range of

Olympic Ring

The Olympic Ring on Montjuïc was the main site of the 1992 Games. It comprises the Olympic Stadium, the Palau Sant Jordi, the Picornell swimming pools, the Institut Nacional d'Educació Física and an eye-catching communications tower which are set out along a classically designed avenue. These facilities continue to host sporting events and musicals.

Museums

MUSEU OLÍMPIC I DE L'ESPORT
Av. de l'Estadi, 60→ **4.2** C2
www.museuolimpicbcn.cat
A pioneering museum in Europe and a showcase for sport with multimedia and interactive exhibits.

MUSEU D'ARQUEOLOGIA DE CATALUNYA
Pg. Santa Madrona, 39-41 →**4.2** C1
T 93 423 21 49
www.mac.cat
The Graphic Arts Pavilion built for the 1929 International Exhibition is home to the MAC's collections tracing the roots of Catalonia, from prehistoric times to the medieval era.

MUSEU ETNOLÒGIC
Pg. Santa Madrona, 16-22 →**4.2** C1
www.museuetnologic.bcn.cat
Collection of ethnographic materials from around the world.

JARDÍ BOTÀNIC
Dr. Font i Quer, 2 →**4.2** B2
www.jardibotanic.bcn.cat
Groundbreaking landscape design preserving Mediterranean plants from around the world.

Restaurants, bars and...

Poble-sec is home to typical taverns and bars full of the flavour and charm of the neighbourhood, including **La Bodegueta del Poble-sec** (Blai, 47 →**4.2** D1), **Taverna Can Margarit** (Concòrdia, 21 →**4.2** D1), **La Tomaquera** (Margarit, 58 →**4.2** D1) and **El Sortidor** (Pl. del Sortidor, 5 →**4.2** D1).

LA BELLA NAPOLI
Margarit, 14 →**4.2** D1
T 93 442 50 56
(15-30 €)
Wood-oven-baked pizzas and Neapolitan food prepared by the Naples-born owners.

MONTJUÏC EL XALET
Av. de Miramar, 31 →**4.2** D2
T 93 324 92 70
(50-60 €) + GROUP MENU
Mediterranean cuisine with a view: panoramic terrace and revolving restaurant.

TINTA ROJA
Creu del Molers, 17 →**4.2** D1
T 93 443 32 43
Drinks. Buenos Aires-style décor. Tango classes.

Shops

Poble-sec (→ 4.2 D1) is full of typical local shops. Interesting souvenirs and gifts at the Museu Olímpic i de l'Esport shop.

And also

PISCINES PICORNELL
Av. de l'Estadi, 30-38 →**4.2** B1
The only swimming pool in BCN which has special opening times for naturists. Hydromassage service, sauna... (www.picornell.cat/serveis/nudista.asp).

SCULPTURE CHANGE
Pierre de Coubertin, s/n →**4.2** B1
This sculpture by Aiko Miyawaki comprises 36 cement cylinders crowned by metal rings and steel cables which reflect back the light, especially at dusk.

ATHLETES' FOOTPRINTS
Av. de l'Estadi, 60 →**4.2** C2
Olympic champions and world-famous athletes have left the imprint of their sports shoes in circular paving stones.

JARDINS DE MOSSÈN CINTO VERDAGUER
Av. Miramar, 30 →**4.2** D2
They feature a wealth of plants, trees and water features which flow down the different levels bounded by several terraces.

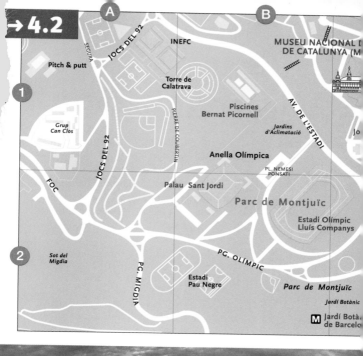

Pitch & putt

SEGURA

JOCS DEL 92

INEFC

MUSEU NACIONAL D
DE CATALUNYA (M

Torre de
Calatrava

1

Grup
Can Clos

JOCS DEL 92

PIERRE DE COUBERTIN

AV. DE L'ESTADI

Piscines
Bernat Picornell

Jardins
d'Aclimatació

Jo

Anella Olímpica

PL. NEMESI
PONSATI

FOC

Palau Sant Jordi

Parc de Montjuïc

Estadi Olímpic
Lluís Companys

2

Sot del
Migdia

PG. MIGDIA

PG. OLÍMPIC

Estadi
Pau Negre

Parc de Montjuïc

Jardí Botànic

M Jardí Botà.
de Barcelo

Olympic Ring →4.2 B1

Jardí Botànic →4.2 B2

Castle + Miramar

The sea-facing side of Montjuïc Hill is the perfect place to stroll and enjoy the views. It begins at the port, between the exotic Costa i Llobera Gardens, and the Miramar is the first, breathtaking viewing point overlooking the Mediterranean. There are even more spectacular views from the top of Montjuïc, around the castle which is surrounded by the Verdaguer, Petra Kelly and Botanical Gardens.

Montjuïc Cemetery Trail

Dreams of Barcelona is the name of the free guided tour of 40 tombs, including mausoleums and sculptures of great artistic value made by architects and sculptors between 1888 and 1936 in a variety of artistic styles, including *modernista*, neo-Egyptian, neo-Gothic and realist. Calendar: second and fourth Sunday in the month. Times: 11am.
www.cbsa.es

Museums

REFUGI 307
Nou de la Rambla, 169
→ **4.3** C1
www.museuhistoria.bcn.cat
Built by the local residents in 1937 to protect themselves from the bombings by fascist planes during the Spanish Civil War.

CENTRE INTERNACIONAL PER LA PAU
Castell de Motjuïc → **4.3** B2
The International Centre for Peace hosts a permanent exhibition about its future.

Restaurants

ELCHE
Vila i Vilà, 71 → **4.3** D2
T 93 441 30 89
(30-40 €) + GROUP MENU
Time-honoured restaurant. Seafood and Valencian cuisine. Excellent rice dishes.

QUIMET & QUIMET
Poeta Cabanyes, 25 → **4.3** C1
T 93 442 31 42
(30-40 €)
Fourth generation serving delicious tapas in this tiny bar.

ROSAL 34
Roser, 34 → **4.3** C1
T 93 324 90 46
(30-40 €)
Modern yet cosy bar serving signature tapas.

Cafés and bars

Top of Montjuïc
There are snack bars and terraces at the Mirador de l'Alcalde and next to the castle where you can have a drink and a bite to eat.

Poble-sec:
GRAN BODEGA SALTÓ
Blesa, 36 → **4.3** C1
Century-old bar refurbished with exquisite taste. Wines, music, theatre...

PETIT APOLO
Vilà i Vilà, 62 → **4.3** C2
Unique beer hall: each table has its own beer pump. Amount consumed displayed on screens.

SALA APOLO
Nou de la Rambla, 113
→ **4.3** D1
Guest DJs from top nightclubs on the Paral·lel: Nitsa (Friday and Saturday); Canibal (Wednesday) Powder Room (Thursday) and Nasty Mondays (Monday).

And also

CAMÍ DE MAR
→ **4.3** C2 A2
A pleasant 20-minute walk from the Mirador de l'Alcalde to the Mirador del Migdia, which boasts magnificent views of the city, port and Llobregat Delta, with benches in the shade of the castle walls, monuments, including the sculpture dedicated to the metric system, and picnic area when you reach the Mirador del Migdia.

SALA MONTJUÏC
Open-air cinema at the castle with recliners and picnics. In summer only.

JARDINS DE MOSSÈN COSTA I LLOBERA
→ **4.3** C2
On the southern slope of Montjuïc, overlooking the sea, a fine collection of cacti and succulent plants.

JARDINS DE JOAN BROSSA
→ **4.3** C1
Part woodland, part garden with three children's play areas.

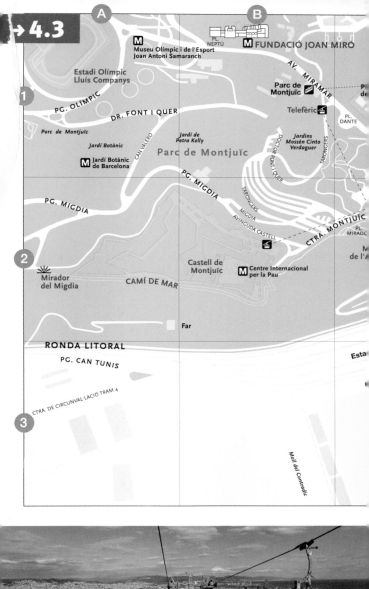

→4.3

A **B**

PL. NEPTÚ

M FUNDACIÓ JOAN MIRÓ

M
Museu Olímpic i de l'Esport
Joan Antoni Samaranch

AV. MIRAMAR

Estadi Olímpic
Lluís Companys

Parc de
Montjuïc

P
de

1

PG. OLÍMPIC

DR. FONT I QUER

Telefèric

PL.
DANTE

Parc de Montjuïc

Jardí de
Petra Kelly

Jardí Botànic

Parc de Montjuïc

M Jardí Botànic
de Barcelona

CAN VALERO

Jardins
Mossèn Cinto
Verdaguer

DOCTOR FONT I QUER

TARONGERS

PG. MIGDIA

PG. MIGDIA

TARONGERS

MIGDIA

AVINGUDA CASTELL

CTRA. MONTJUÏC

PL.
MIRADO

2

Mirador
del Migdia

CAMÍ DE MAR

Castell de
Montjuïc

M Centre Internacional
per la Pau

M
de l'A

Far

RONDA LITORAL

PG. CAN TUNIS

Esta

CTRA. DE CIRCUNVAL·LACIÓ TRAM 4

3

Moll del Contradic

33 **Montjuïc cable car →4.3**C1

The face of the future

22@ is Barcelona's new technology district and an absolute must for anyone wanting to discover the future face of the city. 22@ stretches along the Diagonal from the Plaça de les Glòries to the sea, and stands on a site in Poblenou which is equivalent to 115 blocks. This area was the city's industrial hub in the 19th century and has now become a compact neighbourhood: it is home to industries associated with new technologies, the audiovisual sector, information, communication and biomedicine, which are combined with office blocks, housing, university buildings and other services. The buildings in 22@ have been designed by some of the most famous contemporary architects.

Don't miss

→ 5 B2 TORRE AGBAR
Avinguda Diagonal, 209-211 | www.torreagbar.com
The Agbar Tower is one of Barcelona's new architectural landmarks. Designed by Jean Nouvel who drew inspiration from the mountains of Montserrat and the basilica of the Sagrada Família, this tapering, cylindrical building stands 144 metres high. It can be seen from all around the city, particularly at night, when it is transformed into an enormous lamp of changing colours. ● p. 75

→ 5 A2 L'AUDITORI / MUSEU DE LA MÚSICA
Lepant, 150 | T 93 247 93 00 | www.auditori.cat
Padilla, 155 | T 93 256 36 50 | www.museumusica.bcn.cat
L'Auditori opened in 1999 and is Barcelona's most complete musical facility. It was designed by Rafael Moneo and has three concert halls, seating 2,200, 600 and 400 people and hosts a busy concert schedule. It is also home to the music school, the Escola Superior de Música de Catalunya, and the Museu de la Música.

→ 5 A2 TEATRE NACIONAL DE CATALUNYA
Plaça de les Arts, 1 | T 93 306 57 00 | www.tnc.cat
Next to L'Auditori, the Teatre Nacional de Catalunya (TNC) is the cultural hub of the Plaça de les Arts. It opened in 1996 and is housed in a classically inspired building by Ricardo Bofill. It stages plays from the classical repertoire as well as works by up-and-coming authors, and combines its own productions with those by companies from around the world, and dance performances with plays for children. It has three theatre venues seating 900, 500 and 300 people.

→ 5 D2 PARC DEL CENTRE DEL POBLENOU
Avinguda Diagonal, 130 | T 93 310 50 94
This is Barcelona's newest park. It opened in spring 2008 and was designed by Jean Nouvel, the architect behind the Agbar Tower. The park stands next to the Diagonal and is a shady oasis of calm in the middle of the city offering a new experience to its visitors. Outstanding features include the different pictorial and sculptural elements that line the paths through the park.

Museums

FUNDACIÓ VILA CASAS. CAN FRAMIS

Roc Boronat, 116 →5 C2
www.fundaciovilacasas.com
Houses a collection of
Catalan painting in two
sections of a former
woollen mill dating from
the 18th century.

Restaurants

There hasn't been
enough time to set up
many restaurants in this
new technology district.
Nevertheless, there are
a few interesting places
to eat, such as **El Pastor**
(Zamora, 78; →5 A3),

the **Megataverna del
Poblenou**, which opens
at lunchtime, and **22Alfa
Restaurant** (Badajoz, 115;
→5 B3), with its
Mediterranean cuisine
with a creative touch.

ELS TRES PORQUETS

Rambla Poblenou, 165
→5 C3
T 93 300 87 50
(20-40 €) + SET LUNCH MENU
New wine bar serving top-
quality tapas.

More than 60 €
DOS CIELOS *
→ P. 88

Cafés and bars

Among the most
interesting are **Pepe Bar**
(Pamplona, 91; →5 A3), a
haven for rock & roll fans,
and some tapas bars,
beer halls and cafés in the
lively Clot neighbourhood:
Celler ca la Paqui (Sant
Joan de Malta, 53; →5 C2),
Donde Pican los Santos
(Aragó, 612; →5 C1), and
Bracafé (Clot, 89; →5 C1).

Shops

Shopping centre:
BARCELONA-GLÒRIES
→ P. 87

Les Corts
Sarrià
Sant Gervasi

The districts of Les Corts and Sarrià-Sant Gervasi are home to some of Barcelona's most sought-after residential neighbourhoods. They have in common their proximity to the Collserola Ridge. Pedralbes, at the top of Les Corts, abuts on the ridge and also has green areas, such as the Parc Cervantes and the gardens of the Royal Palace, the Palau Reial. Sarrià-Sant Gervasi, which includes Vallvidrera, encroaches on Collserola, and more than half of its surface area extends above the upper ring-road, the Ronda de Dalt. Sarrià, the last village to be annexed by Barcelona in the 1920s, retains the structure of its old centre and is still a key central area.

Don't miss

→ 6 A2 PAVELLONS DE LA FINCA GÜELL
Avinguda de Pedralbes, 7 | T 93 204 52 50

The gates outside the Güell Estate are one of Gaudí's most richly imaginative works. They depict a fierce winged dragon, which was originally painted in bright colours, its jaws activated by a mechanical device. This wrought-iron gate leads to the caretaker's lodge and the stables that marked the entrance to the estate, which stood just off the Diagonal. Gaudí's patron, Eusebi Güell, had the estate demolished to make way for the Royal Palace, the Palau Reial. For years, the stables were home to the Càtedra Gaudí, a university research centre, which preserves the architect's legacy.

→ 6 A1 MUSEU-MONESTIR DE PEDRALBES
Baixada del Monestir, 9 | T 93 203 92 82 | www.museuhistoria.bcn.cat

Pedralbes Monastery was built seven centuries ago in uptown Barcelona. Its church and monastic buildings are set out around a beautiful three-tier cloister and are one of the best-preserved examples of Catalan Gothic architecture. The monastery has been home to a community of nuns from the Order of Saint Clare since 1327, and in 1983 opened some of its rooms to the public, which have been converted into museum galleries. The monastery is home to collections of paintings, ceramics, silver and goldware and furniture, as well as the chapel of Sant Miquel, with its murals by Ferrer Bassa. ➕ p. 76

→ 6 A3 CAMP NOU - FC BARCELONA
The 99,000-seater F.C. Barcelona Stadium is one of the great "cathedrals" of world football. Since it opened in 1957, it has witnessed some of Barça's greatest sporting achievements. On match days, it attracts a devoted band of local supporters, who consider it their second home. The stadium welcomes a million visitors a year from the rest of Spain and abroad who are interested in its facilities and museum, which showcases the trophies and memorabilia which have shaped the club's history. ➕ p. 77

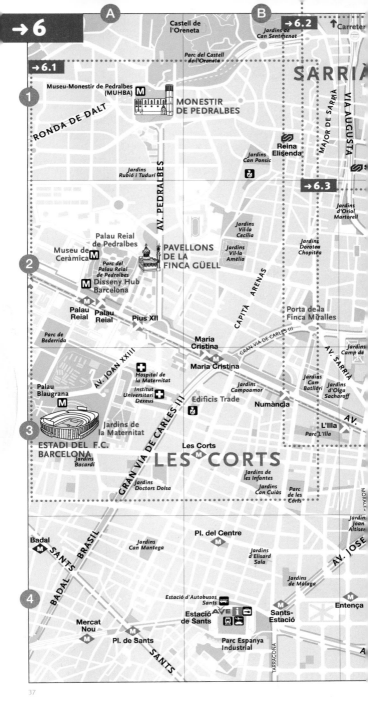

Les Corts

This district comprises the former municipality of Les Corts, Maternitat, Sant Ramon and Pedralbes, which flank the Diagonal, the avenue leading out of city. A former agricultural area, Les Corts was irrigated by the streams that flowed down from neighbouring Collserola and still retains a number of green areas thanks to its sports facilities, parks and the aforementioned ridge.

Museums

MUSEU DEL FUTBOL CLUB BARCELONA
Av. Arístides Maillol, gates 7 & 9 →6.1 A4
www.fcbarcelona.cat
A pioneering football museum which attracts over one million visitors every year.

MUSEU DE CERÀMICA
Av. Diagonal, 686 →6.1 B2
www.museuceramica.bcn.cat
Prestigious collection of Spanish ceramics.

Restaurants

More than 60 € → P. 88
NEICHEL *
* Michelin-starred

LA TERTÚLIA
Morales, 15 →6 C3
T 93 419 58 97
(20-40 €) + SET LUNCH MENU
Thought-provoking, market-fresh cuisine in a charming building.

MUSSOL PEDRALBES
Av. Diagonal, 611 →6.1 C3
T 93 410 13 13
(20-30 €) + GROUP MENU
Typical Catalan specialities at affordable prices.

NEGRO-ROJO
Av. Diagonal, 640 →6.1 C3
(35-45 €) + SET LUNCH MENU
T 93 405 94 44
Split-level restaurant serving different specialities. Upstairs, cosmopolitan dishes. Downstairs, Japanese cuisine.

VIVANDA
Major de Sarrià, 134 →6.1 C1
T 93 203 19 18
(30-40 €)
Serves top-quality tapas and dishes. It has a pleasant indoor terrace.

Cafés and bars

FRANKFURT PEDRALBES
Jordi Girona, 4 →6.1 A2
(6-15 €)
Popular with students. Serves great frankfurters.

SANDOR
Plaça de Francesc Macià, 5 →6 C3
Popular with well-heeled locals. Pavement café all year round.

Shops

This area is known for its major shopping centres and department stores and has fewer typical neighbourhood shops.

Shopping centres:
EL CORTE INGLÉS
L'ILLA DIAGONAL
PEDRALBES CENTRE
→ P. 87

BOTIGA FCB
Av. Arístides Maillol, s/n →6.1 A4
Official team strips, fashion, pyjamas, baby clothes, accessories, homeware, etc.

HARLEY DAVIDSON BCN
Joan Güell, 207 →6.1 C4
Dealer for the legendary motorbike, accessories, clothing, servicing and restaurant.

RAIMA
Deu i Mata, 70 →6.1 C4
Stationery set out by colour. A classic.

And also

VIL·LA CECÍLIA AND VIL·LA AMÈLIA
→6.1 C2
These gardens, with their centuries-old trees, are located in the spacious grounds of a former private estate and are an oasis of calm.

PLAÇA LA CONCÒRDIA
→6.1 C4
Together with the Pl. Can Rosés and Pl. Comas, this square is the heart of the former village of Les Corts which was annexed by Barcelona in 1897.

PORTA MIRALLES
→6.1 C3
The Gaudí-designed gate to the estate belonging to his friend Miralles.

PARC DEL CASTELL DE L'ORENETA
→6.1 B1
A large wooded area that links the city to the Collserola Ridge. It has a picnic area and boasts magnificent views of the city. Visitors can go pony trekking and, on Sundays, from 11am to 2pm, they can ride on one of Europe's best miniature trains.

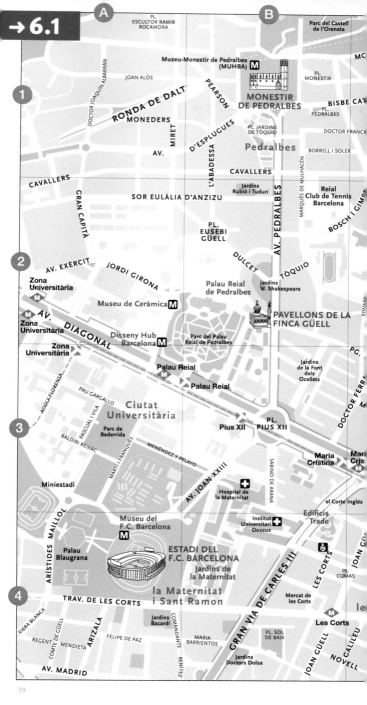

A

B

PL. ESCULTOR RAMIR ROCAMORA

Parc del Castell de l'Oreneta

MO

1

DOCTOR JOAQUÍN ALBARRÁN

JOAN ALÒS

PEARSON

Museu-Monestir de Pedralbes (MUHBA) M

PL. MONESTIR

RONDA DE DALT

MONEDERS

MONESTIR DE PEDRALBES

BISBE CAT

PL. PEDRALBES

MIRET

D'ESPLUGUES

PL. JARDINS DE TÒQUIO

DOCTOR FRANCI

AV.

L'ABADESSA

Pedralbes

BORRELL I SOLER

CAVALLERS

CAVALLERS

GRAN CAPITÀ

SOR EULÀLIA D'ANZIZU

Jardins Rubió i Tudurí

MARQUÈS DE MULHACÉN

AV. PEDRALBES

Reial Club de Tennis Barcelona

BOSCH I GIMP

PL. EUSEBI GÜELL

DULCET

2

Zona Universitària M

AV. EXÈRCIT

JORDI GIRONA

TÒQUIO

Museu de Ceràmica M

Palau Reial de Pedralbes

Jardins W. Shakespeare

M Zona Universitària

AV. DIAGONAL

Zona Universitària

ADOLF FLORENÇA

PAU GARGALLO

Disseny Hub Barcelona M

Parc del Palau Reial de Pedralbes

PAVELLONS DE LA FINCA GÜELL

EDV

PG.

Palau Reial M

Jardins de la Font dels Ocellets

DOCTOR FERR

M

Palau Reial

PASCUAL VILA

Ciutat Universitària

3

BALDIRI REIXAC

Parc de Bederrida

Pius XII

PL. PIUS XII

Maria Cristina

Mari Cris

M

MARTÍ I FRANQUÉS

MENENDEZ Y PELAYO

SABINO DE ARANA

Miniestadi

AV. JOAN XXIII

Hospital de la Maternitat

el Corte Inglés

MAILLOL

Museu del F.C. Barcelona M

Institut Universitari Dexeus

Edificis Trade

ARISTIDES

Palau Blaugrana

ESTADI DEL F.C. BARCELONA

Jardins de la Maternitat

GRAN VIA DE CARLES III

LES CORTS

JOAN GÜ

PL. COMAS

4

ARIZALA

TRAV. DE LES CORTS

la Maternitat i Sant Ramon

Mercat de les Corts

M Les Corts

le

RIERA BLANCA

REGENT MENDIETA

COMTE DE GÜELL

FELIPE DE PAZ

Jardins Bacardí

COMANDANTE BENÍTEZ

MARIA BARRIENTOS

PL. SOL DE BAIX

Jardins Doctors Dolsa

JOAN GÜELL

NOVELL

GALILEU

AV. MADRID

Sarrià + Sant Gervasi

The residential character of the uptown district of Sarrià-Sant Gervasi led to the construction of many detached houses with gardens which have defined its physiognomy for over a century. The imprints of Gaudí and his contemporaries still survive in the area, which has gradually blended into the city's urban layout.

Gaudí Trail

There are two landmarks by this architectural genius in this area. The **Col·legi de les Teresianes**, an austere stone and brick building with a beautiful, light-filled interior, and the **Torre de Bellesguard**, where Gaudí paid his own personal tribute to Catalan Gothic architecture. The interiors are closed to visitors. Download the audioguide *Gaudí's Barcelona* onto your MP3 player (http://bcnshop. barcelonaturisme.com).

Restaurants

More than 60 € → P. 88
ÀBAC *
FREIXA TRADICIÓ
HISOP *
HOFFMAN *
VIA VENETO *

* Michelin-starred

CASA JOANA
Major de Sarrià, 59
→ **6.2** A2
T 93 203 10 36
(20-30 €) + SET LUNCH MENU
Retains the style of an old inn with tasty home-cooking.

CASA FERNÁNDEZ
Santaló, 46 → **6.2** C4
T 93 201 93 08
(40-50 €) + GROUP MENU
Home-cooking and cold and hot tapas until 1am. A wide range of beers.

COURE
Passatge Marimón, 20
→ **6** D3
T 93 200 75 32
(50-60 €)
The chef Albert Ventura produces refined, imaginative cuisine based on traditional Catalan dishes.

FLASH-FLASH
Granada del Penedès, 25
→ **6** D3
T 93 237 09 90
(20-30 €)
Specialises in omelettes. Kitchen open from 1pm to 1am. Pop-art interior design.

IL GIARDINETTO
Granada del Penedès, 22
→ **6** D3
T 93 218 75 36
(40-50 €) + SET LUNCH MENU
Decorated like a garden. Serves excellent Italian cuisine.

L'OLIANA
Santaló, 54 → **6.2** C4
T 93 201 06 47
(45-55 €) + GROUP MENU
Time-honoured Catalan cuisine in an elegant, light-filled setting.

Cafés and bars

BAR TOMÁS
Major de Sarrià, 49 → **6.2** A2
Neighbourhood bar which many consider serves the city's best spicy potatoes.

DOLE
Manuel de Falla, 16-18
→ **6.1** C2
Very small bar specializing in omelettes with a loyal local clientele.

Shops

PASTISSERIA FOIX
Major de Sarrià, 57 → **6.2** A2
Pl. de Sarrià, 12-13
Since 1886. It has made cakes for royal weddings and sends its products around the world.

PUIG DORIA
Av. Diagonal, 612 → **6** C3
Innovative, top-of-the-range designer jewellery for more than 50 years.

JOFRÉ
Bori i Fontestà, 2-6 → **6.2** B4
Leading international fashion brands for ladies and children.

And also

JARDINS TERAPÈUTICS DE VIL·LA FLORIDA
Muntaner, s/n → **6.2** C2
A therapeutic journey featuring two classic treatments: footbaths and textured mats.

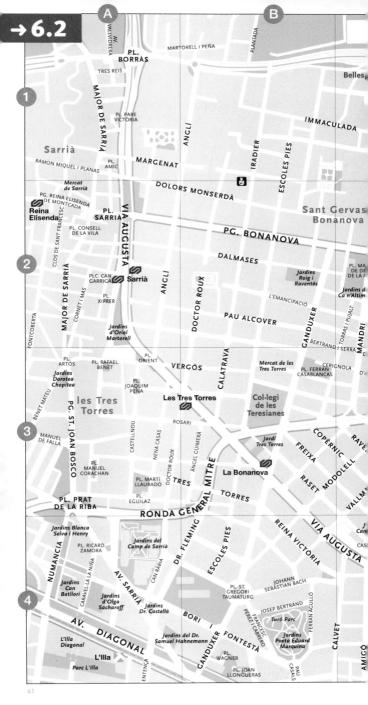

A B

1

PL. BORRÀS

AV. VALLVIDRERA

MARTORELL I PEÑA

TRES REIS

MAJOR DE SARRIÀ

PL. PARE VICTÒRIA

PLANTADA

Belles

IMMACULADA

Sarrià

RAMON MIQUEL I PLANAS

PL. AMIC

MARGENAT

ANGLÍ

IRADIER

ESCOLES PIES

DOLORS MONSERDÀ

Mercat de Sarrià

PG. REINA ELISENDA DE MONTCADA

Reina Elisenda

PL. CONSELL DE LA VILA

PL. SARRIÀ

VIA AUGUSTA

PG. BONANOVA

Sant Gervasi Bonanova

2

CLOS DE SANT FRANCESC

MAJOR DE SARRIÀ

CORNET I MAS

PLC. CAN GARRIGA

Sarrià

PL. XIPRER

ANGLÍ

DALMASES

DOCTOR ROUX

Jardins Roig i Raventós

PL. MA DE DE DE LA F

L'EMANCIPACIÓ

Jardins de Ca n'Altim

PAU ALCOVER

GANDUXER

TORRAS I PUJALT

MANDRI

FONTCOBERTA

Jardins d'Oriel Martorell

PL. ORIENT

BERTRAND I SERRA

PL. ARTÓS

PL. RAFAEL BENET

VERGÓS

CALATRAVA

Mercat de les Tres Torres

CERIGNOLA
PL. FERRAN CASABLANCAS

D'A

Jardins Dorotea Chopitea

PL. JOAQUIM PEÑA

Les Tres Torres

Col·legi de les Teresianes

3

BENET MATEU

les Tres Torres

PG. ST. JOAN BOSCO

CASTELLNOU

NENA CASAS

ROSARI

DOCTOR ROUX

ÀNGEL GUIMERÀ

Jardí Tres Torres

COPÈRNIC

FREIXA

RAVE

MANUEL DE FALLA

PL. MANUEL CORACHAN

La Bonanova

RASET

MODOLELL

PL. MARTÍ LLAURADÓ

TRES

MITRE

TORRES

VALLM

PL. PRAT DE LA RIBA

PL. EGUILAZ

RONDA GENERAL

REINA VICTÒRIA

VIA AUGUSTA

J Can

4

NUMÀNCIA

Jardins Blanca Selva i Henry

PL. RICARD ZAMORA

CARAVEL·LA LA NIÑA

Jardins del Camp de Sarrià

CAN RABIA

DR. FLEMING

ESCOLES PIES

CAS

Jardins Can Batllori

Jardins d'Olga Sacharoff

AV. SARRIÀ

Jardins Dr. Castelló

PL. ST. GREGORI TAUMATURG

JOHANN SEBASTIAN BACH

JOSEP BERTRAND

FRANCESC PÉREZ I CABRERO

FERRAN AGULLÓ

CALVET

L'Illa Diagonal

AV. DIAGONAL

ENTENÇA

Jardins del Dr. Samuel Hahnemann

BORI I

GANDUXER

FONTESTÀ

PL. WAGNER

Turó Parc

Jardins Poeta Eduard Marquina

PAU CASALS

AMIGÓ

L'Illa

Parc L'Illa

PL. JOAN LLONGUERAS

41

Collserola

The Parc de Collserola is Barcelona's vast "green lung", an area of forest which winds its way from the Besòs to the Llobregat rivers, and separates the city from the county of the Vallès. Parts of the park have been built on, but it has been a protected area since 1987, allowing it to preserve most of its Mediterranean woodland, comprising pines, ilexes and oaks, and fauna, which ranges from rabbits to wild boars.

Museums

MUSEU D'AUTÒMATES DEL TIBIDABO
Plaça del Tibidabo, 3-4
➔ **6.3** D1
www.tibidabo.es
An amazing collection of automata, some of them from the 19th century.

Restaurants

LA MASIA
Plaça Tibidabo, s/n ➔ **6.3** C1
T 93 417 63 50
(20-30 €)
Catalan recipes with a modern twist.

LA VENTA
Plaça Doctor Andreu, s/n
➔ **6.3** D3
T 93 212 64 55
(35-45 €) + GROUP MENU
A short but mouthwatering menu of Catalan dishes. Housed in a *modernista* building.

L'ORANGERIE
Cta. de Vallvidrera al Tibidabo, 83-93 ➔ **6.3** D1
T 93 259 30 00
(+60 €) + SET LUNCH MENU
Charming restaurant serving creative signature cuisine. Spectacular views.

Cafés and bars
A cluster of BCN classics with stunning city views which are the perfect place for a relaxing drink.

BAR MIRAMAR
Hotel La Florida ➔ **6.3** D1
Modern and relaxed atmosphere on the terrace and by the hotel pool.

DANZATORIA
Av. Tibidabo, 61 ➔ **6.3** D2
Housed in a 19th-century villa. Two levels with different areas and a beautiful garden.

MERBEYÉ
Plaça Doctor Andreu, s/n
➔ **6.3** D3
With original design by Mariscal, it has altered little since it opened. A cosy place at any time of day.

MIRABLAU
Plaça Doctor Andreu, 2
➔ **6.3** D3
Bar overlooking the city. Two levels and a terrace with excellent service.

And also

VALLVIDRERA
Neighbourhood at the top of Collserola. Highlights include the church of Santa Maria built between 1570 and 1587 in the late-Gothic style on the site of the original church dating from 987 AD.

DINNER UNDER THE STARS
Observatori Fabra ➔ **6.3** C2
T 93 847 95 08
From June to September, dinners in the gardens of the Fabra Observatory (1904). Includes a guided tour and the chance to watch the night sky.
www.observatorifabra.com

Off the map:

LES PLANES
Popular with BCN locals for Sunday outings, with its snack bars and barbecues. 20 min. from Pl. Catalunya on Catalan railways (FGC).

CENTRE D'INTERPRETACIÓ DEL PARC DE COLLSEROLA
Crta. Vallvidrera-Sant Cugat, km 4.7
Exhibition about the flora and fauna in the natural park.

Tibidabo funicular

Les Planes

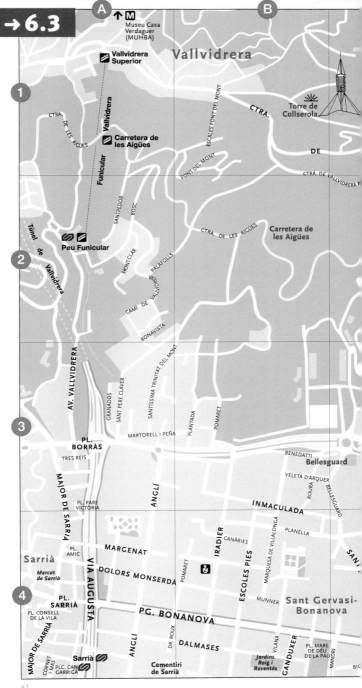

A　**B**

↑ **M** Museu Casa Verdaguer (MUHBA)

Vallvidrera Superior

Vallvidrera

CTRA.

Torre de Collserola

CTRA. DE LES AIGÜES

Funicular

Vallvidrera

Carretera de les Aigües

DE

ESCOLES FONT DEL MONT

FONT DEL MONT

CTRA. DE VALLVIDRERA

SANTPEDOR

BOSC

CTRA. DE LES AIGÜES

Carretera de les Aigües

Peu Funicular

Túnel de Vallvidrera

MONTCLAR

PALAFOLLS

CAMÍ DE VALLVIDRERA

CAMÍ DE VALLVIDRERA

BONAVISTA

AV. VALLVIDRERA

GRANADOS

SANT PERE CLAVER

SANTÍSSIMA TRINITAT DEL MONT

PLANTADA

POMARET

PL. BORRÀS

MARTORELL I PEÑA

TRES REIS

Bellesguard

BENEDATTI

VELETA D'ARQUER

ROURA

BELLESGUARD

MAJOR DE SARRIÀ

ANGLÍ

PL. PARE VICTÒRIA

INMACULADA

MARGENAT

IRADIER

CANÀRIES

PLANELLA

Sarrià

PL. AMIC

ESCOLES PIES

MARQUESA DE VILLALONGA

Mercat de Sarrià

VIA AUGUSTA

DOLORS MONSERDA

POMARET

MUNNER

Sant Gervasi-Bonanova

PL. SARRIÀ

PL. CONSELL DE LA VILA

PG. BONANOVA

ANGLÍ

DR. ROUX

DALMASES

VILANA

GANDUXER

PL. MARE DE DÉU DE LA PAU

MANDRI

MAJOR DE SARRIÀ

CORNET I MAS

PL. CAN GARRIGA

Sarrià

Cementiri de Sarrià

Jardins Roig i Raventós

BIC

Horta + Guinardó

The district of Horta-Guinardó winds its way up the Collserola Ridge, between Gràcia and Nou Barris. It is subdivided into 11 neighbourhoods and forms a border between the urban layout of the city and nature. It has large swathes of green, which include the whole area above the upper ring-road, the Ronda de Dalt, which encroaches on Collserola, part of the Vall d'Hebron and Carmel. Most of the district has uneven landform and sloping terrain, and boasts major healthcare and sporting facilities, as well as places where the pace of life is more relaxed, such as the former village of Horta.

Don't miss

→ 7 D1 PARC DEL LABERINT D'HORTA

Germans Desvalls, s/n | T 93 428 25 00

This neo-classical-style garden with its romantic atmosphere is located at the foot of the Collserola Ridge. It features fountains, ponds and canals, and its architecture and sculptures combine with unusual plant species. Its centrepiece is the intricate cypress maze. The garden was built for one of the city's aristocratic families and opened to the public in 1971.

→ 7 C2 PAVELLÓ DE LA REPÚBLICA

Cardenal Vidal i Barraquer, s/n | www.ub.es/cehi/elpavel.php

In 1937, at the height of the Civil War, Spain opened its pavilion at the Paris World Fair. The pioneering building, designed by Josep Lluís Sert and Luis Lacasa, was used to present Pablo Picasso's *Guernica*, and works by Joan Miró, Julio González, Alberto Sánchez and Alexander Calder. A faithful replica of the building was built in Horta in 1992, as the headquarters for the study centre, the Centre d'Estudis Històrics Internacionals.

→ 7 A3 PARC DE LA CREUETA DEL COLL

Pg. Mare de Déu del Coll, s/n

The Parc de la Creueta del Coll was built on the site of a disused quarry and offers amenities for all ages. Highlights include the large swimming pool, with Eduardo Chillida's 54-tonne monumental concrete sculpture *In Praise of Water* recreating the legend of Narcissus, suspended over the far end from four thick steel cables.

Museums

MUSEU DE CARRUATGES DEL FOMENT

Pl. Josep Pallach, 8 → 7 C

Carts, carriages, wagons and clothing and accessories used by coachmen and carters in the 19th and 20th centuries.

Restaurants

CAN CORTADA

Av. Estatut de Catalunya, s/n → 7 D2

T 93 427 23 15

(30-40 €) + GROUP MENU

Mediterranean cuisine and traditional Catalan fare in an 11th-century farmhouse with an attractive garden.

CAN TRAVI NOU

Jorge Manrique, s/n → 7 C2

T 93 428 04 34

(40-50 €) + GROUP MENU

Market-fresh, Catalan cuisine in a setting steeped in the charm of Horta's rural past.

ELS MISTOS

Juan de Mena, 1-3 → 7 C2

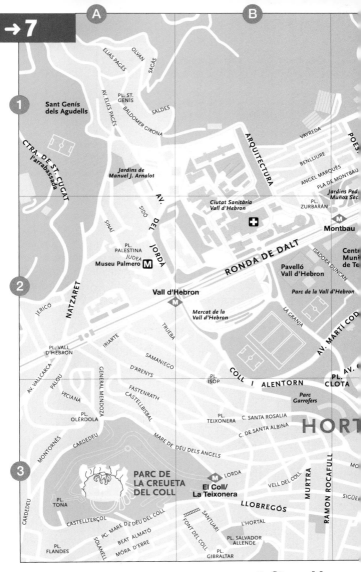

Map labels:

ELIAS PAGÈS
OLVAN
SAGAS
Sant Genís dels Agudells
AV. ELIES PAGÈS
PL. ST. GENÍS
SALDES
BALDOMER GIRONA
CTRA. DE ST. CUGAT
l'arrabassada
Jardins de Manuel J. Arnalot
SINAI
SIDO
AV. DEL JORDA
Ciutat Sanitària Vall d'Hebron
ARQUITECTURA
VAYREDA
BENLLIURE
ANGEL MARQUÈS
PLA DE MONTBAU
POES.
Jardins Ped. Muñoz Sec.
PL. ZURBARÁN
Montbau
PL. PALESTINA
JUDEA
Museu Palmero
RONDA DE DALT
ISADORA DUNCAN
Centre Muni de Te
Pavelló Vall d'Hebron
NATZARET
JERICO
Vall d'Hebron
Mercat de la Vall d'Hebron
Parc de la Vall d'Hebron
LA GRANJA
AV. MARTI COD
PL. VALL D'HEBRON
IRIARTE
TRUEBA
SAMANIEGO
D'ARENYS
COLL I ALENTORN
PL. ISOP
Parc Garrofers
PL. AV. CLOTA
AV. VALLCARCA
PALOU
GENERAL MENDOZA
FASTENRATH
CASTELLBISBAL
VECIANA
PL. OLÈRDOLA
PL. TEIXONERA
C. SANTA ROSALIA
C. DE SANTA ALBINA
HORT
MONTORNÈS
CARDEDEU
MARE DE DÉU DELS ANGELS
PARC DE LA CREUETA DEL COLL
El Coll/ La Teixonera
LORDA
VELL DEL COLL
MURTRA
RAMON ROCAFULL
MO
SIGÜE
PL. TONA
CARDEDEU
CASTELLTERÇOL
PG. MARE DE DÉU DEL COLL
SOLANELL
BEAT ALMATÓ
MÓRA D'EBRE
SANTUARI
FONT DEL COLL
LLOBREGÓS
L'HORTAL
PL. SALVADOR ALLENDE
PL. GIBRALTAR
PL. FLANDES

T 93 428 21 37
(25-40 €)
Excellent, simple food using the finest Galician products.

Off the map:
ADDENDA
Pg. Maragall, 176
T 93 506 44 90
(25-35 €) + SET LUNCH MENU

Traditional Catalan and Spanish cuisine with a French twist.
LA BOTA DEL RACÓ
Mare de Déu de Montserrat, 232
T 93 456 60 01
(30-40 €)
Generous servings of typical Catalan cuisine.

Cafés and bars
BAR QUIMET
Pl. Eivissa, 10 →7 D3
More than 20 varieties of omelette. Good tapas.
CASA FAUSTO
Funoses Llussà, 2 →7 B3
A renovated neighbourhood classic. Meals also served.

Sant Andreu + Nou Barris

Founded over 1,000 years ago, Sant Andreu is one of the traditional gateways to Barcelona. It has a strong industrial past and is currently immersed in a process of transformation, with the laying of the high-speed train track and the construction of the new station at La Sagrera, which will be the city's second high-speed-train terminal. This major rail project will bring about the redevelopment of Sant Andreu and redefine its centrality. The district of Nou Barris is on the other side of the Avinguda Meridiana, which marks the boundary of Sant Andreu, and stretches as far as the foothills of Collserola. This Barcelona district was established relatively recently by successive waves of incomers from the rest of Spain. It also has the most neighbourhoods – there are now 13.

Don't miss

→ 8 A1 PARC CENTRAL DE NOU BARRIS
Pl. de Karl Marx, s/n
The 16-hectare Parc Central de Nou Barris is Barcelona's second biggest park, after the Parc de la Ciutadella. It was begun in the 1990s and is home to the district's main amenities, including the library. Particularly outstanding are the water features and planting. The park has ponds, one of them with waterfalls, and a number of pathways, as well as 30 different species of trees, including willows, poplars, palms, ilexes, acacias...

→ 8 C2 CASA BLOC
Pg. de Torras i Bages, 91-105
The Casa Bloc is a landmark of the most committed rationalist architecture: the first major Spanish workers' housing project which combines 200 private duplexes with communal gardens. The block was designed on a Z-shaped ground plan and designed by the GATCPAC architects – Sert, Torres Clavé, Subirana – in 1932. It soon set the benchmark for progressive architecture. Sadly neglected after the Civil War, it has undergone a major refurbishment to restore its original appearance.

→ 8 C3 FABRA I COATS
Ferran Junoy, 10
The Fabra i Coats project is one of the most ambitious interventions in the municipal policy of converting disused factories into cultural facilities. Over the coming decade, teaching and creativity in fields such as art, music, theatre, dance and audiovisuals will take the baton from the manufacturing processes carried out in this factory from the late-19th to the mid-20th centuries.

Restaurants

CAL TRAGINER
Borriana, 69 →8 B3
T 93 346 48 53
(20-30 €)
Traditional home cooking.
Chargrilled meats and
excellent tapa starters.

HERMANOS TOMÁS
Pare Pérez del Pulgar, 1 →8 B1
T 93 345 71 48
(45-60 €)
Traditional Catalan and
Basque cuisine.

LA PARADETA
Pacífic, 74 →8 B3
T 93 346 48 53
(20-30 €)
Fish chosen from the
counter at the entrance.

L'ESPURNA
Pare Secchi, 21 →8 B2
T 93 311 64 07
(15-25 €) + SET LUNCH MENU
Family-run brasserie and
pizzeria. Home cooking.

MARISQUERIA
DOPAZO
Borriana, 90 →8 B3
T 93 311 47 51
(35-50 €)
Fine Galician seafood for
more than 50 years.

RABASSEDA
Pl. Mercadal, 1 →8 B2
T 93 345 10 17
(25-35 €)
Market-fresh cuisine.
Extremely popular with
locals. Terrace.

TAVERNA CAN ROCA
Gran de Sant Andreu, 209
→8 B2. T 93 346 57 01
(20-30 €) + SET LUNCH MENU
Excellent home-made
soups and stews.

TXAPELDUN
Pg. Fabra i Puig, 159
→8 A2. T 93 352 91 01
(20-30 €) + MID-DAY SET MENU
Basque cuisine. Tapas and
great fish.

Cafés and bars

COLOMBIA
Pg. Fabra i Puig, 1 →8 B3
Bar selling fair-trade
products.

LA ESQUINICA
Fabra i Puig, 296 →8 A1

Barcelona ^{+ info}

Barcelona Cathedral | Museu Picasso | Palau de la Música Catalana |
Museu d'Historia de Barcelona MUHBA | Santa Maria del Mar | Mercat de
la Boqueria | Palau Güell | Museu d'Art Contemporani de Barcelona MACBA |
Reials Drassanes | Museu d'Història de Catalunya MHC | L'Aquàrium |
Frank Gehry's Fish | Museu Blau MCNB | Basílica de la Sagrada Família |
Casa Milà "La Pedrera" | Park Güell | Casa Batlló | Casa Amatller | Fundació
Antoni Tàpies | Hospital de la Santa Creu i Sant Pau | Museu Nacional d'Art
de Catalunya MNAC | Fundació Joan Miró | Mies van der Rohe Pavilion |
CaixaForum - Casaramona Factory | Palau Sant Jordi | Agbar Tower |
Monestir de Pedralbes | Camp Nou - FC Barcelona

Ciutat Vella

Barcelona Cathedral

Opening times
Church only (free):
Monday to Friday: 8am-12.45pm
and 5.15pm-7.30pm. Saturday and
evenings before public holidays:
8am-12.45pm and 5.15pm-8pm.
Sunday and public holidays:
8am-1.45pm and 5.15pm-8pm.
Sightseeing tours
Includes a tour of the church, cloister,
choir, roof and museum (general
admission: 5 €; group with official guide:
3.50 € per person). Monday to Saturday
and evenings before public holidays:

1pm-5pm. Sunday and public holidays:
2pm-5pm

Begun in 1298, the cathedral of the Holy
Cross is one of the most splendid examples of the Catalan Gothic style, which is
characterised by its decorative sobriety
and well-balanced proportions. The
cathedral is an extremely large building
(90 metres long and 40 metres wide),
and was built next to the city walls, at
one end of the medieval city, on the
same site as its two predecessors: the
first cathedral, an early-Christian basilica dating from the 4th century, and the
second, built between 1046 and 1058 in
the Romanesque style.

The construction process was ardu-
ous. To enable people to continue to
worship, the Romanesque cathedral was
gradually dismantled as building work
on the Gothic cathedral progressed,

Barcelona Cathedral

Museu Picasso

culminating in the middle of the 15th century. However, the façade remained unfinished without any towers or sculptural decorations.

Four centuries later, the city hosted the 1888 Universal Exhibition and this triggered the right social and economic conditions that made it possible to complete the building. The neo-Gothic façade was inspired by the original project drawn up by the French master builder Carlí in the 15th century. Its slender lines and abundant decorative elements contrast with the sober horizontal lines of the rest of the building. The two towers flanking either side of the façade were added at a later date.

The east end of the cathedral consists of a single apse with nine radiating chapels that are reached by a wide deambulatory. The crypt is located beneath the high altar and is covered by an almost flat vault consisting of 12 sections. It houses the tomb of Saint Eulalia, one of the patron saints of the city, whose remains lie in an alabaster sarcophagus carved by 14th-century sculptors from Pisa.

The naves of the cathedral are separated from the eastern end of the building by a section with no chapels, which serves as the transept. Two octagonal bell towers surmount either end of this section outside the building. The cathedral is an example of a hall church, meaning that the naves are similar in height. This layout is typical of Catalan Gothic architecture. Made up of four sections, the naves have cross-vaulted ceilings with painstakingly crafted polychrome keystones.

The architects' design was so skilful that, if you look at the ceiling, the building seems to have seven naves instead of three, due to the fact that the ceilings of the side chapels are divided into two small vaults, which are set between buttresses. This intelligent use of space lets in more daylight and gives the interior a highly evocative atmosphere.

The main bell tower with its octagonal base was placed over the section of the central nave closest to the façade: an unusual location in Catalan Gothic buildings. The slender spire at the top, which is the highest point of the building, was built between 1906 and 1913, and was the last major building work carried out on the cathedral.

The lavishly sculpted stone choir, which was created between the late 14th century and mid-16th century, is located in the centre of the great nave, and spans two sections of the cathedral. The wooden stalls inside the choir are a masterpiece of Gothic sculpture.

The great cloister, which was built between the late-14th and early-15th centuries, adjoins the west wall of the cathedral and is reached from the transept. It is rectangular in shape and has four galleries that appear to have cross-vaulted ceilings underpinned by pointed arches, like the naves inside the building. There is a secluded garden in the centre with a pond where 13 geese swim. The number 13 stands for the age of Saint Eulàlia when she was martyred.

Every year, for Corpus Christi, a hollowed-out egg is placed on the water jet of the Gothic fountain in the cloister, in one of the city's most deeply rooted and popular traditions. It is said that if the egg remains balanced on the stream of water throughout the day, the year will be prosperous.

The Blessed Sacrament Chapel or Chapter House is located next to one of the wings of the cloister. It has an extraordinary star-shaped octagonal vault that was built during the early 15th century.

Museu Picasso

Opening times
Tuesday to Sunday (including public holidays): 10am-8pm. Last admissions 30 minutes before closing. Mondays, except public holidays: closed. Annual closing: 1st January, 1st May, 24th June, 25th and 26th December. Admission: Museum+temporary exhibition: 9 €.

Guided tours
For individual visitors, who have pre-booked by phone (T 93 256 30 22) or e-mail (museupicasso@bcn.cat): Catalan (Tuesday 6.30pm and Sunday 1pm, except for the first Sunday in the month); Spanish (Tuesday 5.30pm and Sunday 11.30am); English (Tuesday 4.30pm and Thursday 5.30pm); French (Thursday 4pm)

Carrer Montcada, in the district of La Ribera, is short and narrow, yet despite its appearance it is one of the city's most important streets. Its importance stems from the fact that it was home to Barcelona's nobility for 500 years, from the 13th to the 18th centuries. This explains why the street is a succession of Gothic palazzos of great architectural value.

Five of these palazzos, which stand side by side on the east side of the street, house the Museu Picasso, one of the city's main cultural attractions. The five palazzos – the Palau Aguilar, the Palau del Baró de Castellet, the Palau Meca, the Casa Mauri and the Palau Finestres – were built between the 13th and 14th centuries in the Gothic style and remodelled over the centuries with the addition of Renaissance, baroque and neoclassical elements. They all have the same layout: the rooms are set out around a courtyard with a monumental staircase that leads to the first floor.

Pablo Ruiz Picasso arrived in Barcelona with his family in 1895 when he was barely 14. His father was a schoolteacher. The young Picasso's artistic spirit was forged in the *modernista* ambiance of the Catalan capital, and he lived here for nine years until he left for Paris in 1904.

Picasso retained strong emotional ties with the city throughout the rest of his life and this is why, in 1960, he gave his wholehearted support to the idea mooted by his personal secretary, Jaume Sabartés, to create a museum devoted to his work in Barcelona. The Museu Picasso opened in 1963 and housed Sabartés, personal collection and works by the Malaga-born artist that were on show at the time in different Barcelona galleries. Over the years, the museum's holdings have expanded to include works from other private collections and works donated by Picasso himself.

Highlights include *Motherhood* (1903), *Portrait of Señora Canals* (1905), *Harlequin* (1917) and the series *Las Meninas*, in which the artist dissects Diego de Velázquez's famous painting into 58 oils ranging from a general view to detailed studies.

Palau de la Música Catalana

Guided tours
Daily. Length: 50'
Prices: 12 € (adults); 10 € (students, senior citizens from the EU and groups from 25 people upwards).

Tickets can be purchased at the ticket office, by phone (T 902 475 485) and e-mail (visites@palaumusica.org)

English: 10am, 11am, 12 noon, 1pm, 2pm, 3pm; August and Holy Week: 10am, 11am, 12 noon, 1pm, 2pm, 3pm, 4pm, 5pm, 6pm
Catalan: 10.30am and 12.30pm
Spanish: 11.30am, 1.30pm, 2.30pm, 5.30pm; August and Holy Week: 11.30am, 1.30pm, 2.30pm, 5.30pm, 4.30pm, 5.30pm

Built between 1905 and 1908, at the height of the *modernista* building boom in Barcelona, the Palau de la Música Catalana is, together with the Hospital de Sant Pau, the masterpiece of Lluís Domènech i Montaner, one of the key figures of Catalan art nouveau, or *modernisme*.

The Palau is a UNESCO World Heritage Site and Barcelona's most popular concert hall. It was built on the site of the former convent in the district of Sant Pere, as an initiative of the Orfeó Català, the choral society founded in 1891 to carry out important work in disseminating choral music from Catalonia, the rest of Spain and abroad.

Domènech i Montaner's project was paid for by public subscription, including large donations from industrialists who had made their fortunes over the previous decades. It is an ingenious combination of architecture – made from steel and brick – and a bold use of the applied arts, particularly sculptures, stained glass and ceramics. The Palau is a large rationalist structure whose stability made it possible to free up floors and walls in order to gain space that would make it possible to create the perfect acoustics and add a large amount of decorative details that add colour and vibrancy to the ensemble.

Inside, the building is almost entirely clad in ceramics, with a predominance of floral motifs. Against this colourful backdrop, a series of sculptures protrudes from the walls using an original artistic device that was typical of the fantasy of *modernista* art: the busts of some of the figures are sculpted in relief while the rest of the body is flat and blends into the coloured mosaic.

A German pipe organ dating from 1908 graces the stage, which is flanked by two monumental sculptural ensembles by Pablo Gargallo: one alludes to Catalan folk music and features the bust of one of its key revivalists, the musician Josep Anselm Clavé, and below it an allegory of the

Catalan folk song *Les flors de maig* (The Flowers of May), which he wrote. The second sculptural group portrays international composers and includes a bust of Beethoven and scenes depicting Richard Wagner's Valkyries.

To allow natural light into the 2,000-seat auditorium, Domènech i Montaner had it covered by an enormous, rectangular stained-glass skylight. Its centrepiece is an inverted dome that is suspended like a droplet of water about to fall.

Other impressive areas inside the Palau de la Música include the spacious foyer, with its massive pillars and vaulted ceiling, which separates the entrance and the concert hall, and the Lluís Millet hall on the first floor, where concert-goers meet before a performance, which is lit by a large stained-glass window.

The exterior of the building is just as sumptuous as the interior. Domènech used brick as the main building material and added coloured ceramics and sculptures as the main decorative elements. The architect chose to round off the corner of the outer walls overlooking the Carrer de Sant Pere and the Carrer de Amadeu Vives and surmounted it with a small dome on the roof. The corner also features a large sculptural ensemble – an allegory to Catalan song by Miquel Blay– at first-floor level.

The base of the façade features robust colonnades that underpin broad and low elliptical arches which lead inside the building. A long balcony runs from the first arch along the main façade forming a complex structure of columns that lends its great depth. Above these columns are busts of Palestrina, Bach, Beethoven and Wagner, who represent different periods in the history of music.

From 1982 until 2008, the centenary year of the Palau, the architect Òscar Tusquets supervised restoration and extension work that opened up new views of the building with the demolition of the church of Sant Francesc de Paula and the addition of a new plaza that gives the building a feeling of space.

Museu d'Història de Barcelona MUHBA

Opening times
Tuesday to Saturday: 10am-5pm (November to March) and 10am-7pm (April to October)
Sunday: 10-8pm (admission free from 3pm)
Closed Monday. Annual closing: 1st January, 1st May, 24th June and 25th December
Prices: 7 €; 5 € for the under 25s, over 65s and disabled visitors; admission free for under 16s

Although its collections are distributed among several landmark buildings in the city, the main premises of the Museu d'Història de Barcelona are in the Plaça del Rei, and reached through the Casa Padellàs, a late-15th-century Gothic pal-

Palau de la Música Catalana

Museu d'Història de Barcelona

Barcelona +info

azzo that was moved, stone by stone, from Carrer dels Mercaders when the Via Laietana was being built in 1931.

While the Casa Padellàs was being relocated to the site, archaeologists discovered, below the square, the well-preserved streets and the foundations of the buildings of Roman and medieval Barcino that span the 1st century BC and 13th century AD.

The museum opened in 1943 and one of the main attractions is to take a walk underground, along the streets of the Roman and medieval city with its fountains and drainage systems, touch its ancient walls, admire the mosaic fragments of its shops and factories and realise the importance of the Church on society at the time through the magnitude of its religious centre while noticing that different periods in history are buried in layers just a few metres under the city where we walk today.

The visit to the MUHBA is completed by two major architectural landmarks that are part of the Palau Reial Major: the Great Hall, the Saló del Tinell, and the chapel of Santa Àgata. The Palau Reial Major was the official residence of the Counts of Barcelona and subsequently the kings of the Crown of Aragon, and has been remodelled several times since the 11th century.

The Tinell is the biggest hall in the palace and was built between 1359 and 1370, during the reign of Pere the Ceremonious. A large number of rooms were demolished to build the hall which covers an area of 33 × 18 metres and

has a flat ceiling underpinned by broad, semi-circular arches.

The chapel of Santa Àgata now stands atop the city's medieval walls between the Plaça del Rei and the Plaça de Ramon Berenguer III, on the Via Laietana. It was built on the orders of King Jaume II of Aragon as the oratory of the Palau Reial and was begun in 1302.

With its elegant, airy Gothic forms, the chapel has a single nave covered by a wooden pitched ceiling underpinned by pointed arches and reinforced, like the Tinell, with solid buttresses. The slender octagonal tower is its most eye-catching feature from the outside and one of the main landmarks on Barcelona's medieval skyline.

Santa Maria del Mar

Opening times
Monday to Saturday: 9am-1.30pm and 4.30pm-8pm
Sunday and public holidays: 10.30am-1.30pm and 4.30pm-8pm

From the late 10th century onwards, Barcelona's growing population began to spread beyond the narrow confines of the walled Roman city. The merchants, shipwrights and stevedores, and other trades associated with commerce and harbour life, moved to the east of the city, between the city walls and the sea. Before the new millennium, these guilds had built the church of Santa Maria de les Arenes near the beach, to meet the religious needs of the new town known as Vila Nova del Mar, which was later absorbed by Barcelona as the district of La Ribera.

La Ribera enjoyed a period of great splendour as a result of the large-scale economic development of Barcelona and the Crown of Aragon during the 13th and 14th centuries. The building of Carrer Montcada provided ample proof of this. Crammed with palazzos, the street became the home of the new merchant classes who were vying with the Italian states to gain control of Mediterranean commerce. Further proof of this prosperity was the building of a new church on the site of Santa Maria de les Arenes. It was to be called Santa Maria del Mar, and was built in the Gothic style that was so widespread throughout Europe during the late Middle Ages. The church competed in size with Barcelona Cathedral and

Santa Maria del Mar

showed the strength of the new bourgeois class that was funding it.

So great was their economic power that Santa Maria del Mar, or the *cathedral of the sea* as it soon came to be known, was completed in little more than 50 years. This was an extremely short period in which to build a great Gothic church as projects of this kind usually took centuries to complete. Santa Maria del Mar was begun in 1329, the year of the conquest of the island of Sardinia, which completed the dominance of the western Mediterranean by the Catalan-Aragonese Crown. It was finished in 1383, with only the two bell towers that stand on either side of the main façade remaining unbuilt. One of these was completed in 1496 and the other in 1902.

The fact that Santa Maria del Mar was built over such a short period of time lends it a great stylistic unity, which is the result of the involvement of relatively few master builders. This explains why the church is taken as a paradigmatic example of Catalan Gothic art, characterised by sober decorative elements – which make it easier to distinguish the purely architectural features from the decorative ones; by the profusion of horizontal lines as opposed to the radical vertical lines of the International Gothic style; by the predominance of solid panels over empty spaces in the walls and the choice of the *hall-style* layout in which the side naves and central nave are of equal or similar height, creating flat roofs, a radically different model to the French Gothic and European styles. At Santa Maria del Mar, the buttresses that help support these powerful walls create 12 small chapels in each of the side naves.

Another unusual characteristic of the church is the 13-metre span between the columns: the broadest in a Gothic building. The nave is more than 50 metres wide and is divided into just four sections, highlighting the slenderness of the sparsely decorated octagonal columns which stand 18 metres high. The side naves are half as wide as the central nave, and this accentuates the balance and harmony of the church interior.

In the east end of the church, however, the distance between the columns is drastically reduced in order to separate the deambulatory from the altar, creating an evocative forest of columns that contrasts with the feeling of space in the rest of the church.

Images of Saint Peter and Saint Paul occupy niches on either side of the west door on the main façade. At the top, our attention is drawn to the magnificent rose window which allows light to flood into the church from midday to dusk. The original stained glass in the rose window fell out as a result of the earthquake in 1428 which killed 22 people. The window was replaced at the end of the 15th century by glassmakers working in the Flamboyant style and it is the one we can see today.

Most of the decorative elements inside the church (including the Gothic choir stalls, the baroque high altar and the huge 18th-century pipe organ) were completely destroyed by a fire in 1936 during the days just after the outbreak of the Spanish Civil War.

Mercat de la Boqueria

Opening times
Monday to Saturday: 8am-8.30pm
Closed Sunday

Barcelona's extensive network of well-tended fresh food markets, which can ably compete with modern hypermarkets, set the city apart from most major cities in the west. The market of Sant Josep, better known as the Boqueria, is the jewel in the crown of the 39 markets in the network. Covering an area of 6,000 square metres, it is Spain's biggest fresh-food market and one of the main ingredients

La Boqueria

of the great culinary prestige Barcelona enjoys today.

Its origins can be traced back to the itinerant open-air market that established itself outside the city walls, on La Rambla, in front of the gate of Santa Eulàlia, or La Boqueria, from the end of the 13th century. However, permanent premises weren't built until the middle of the 19th century to cater to the hundreds of stalls selling meat, fish, fruit, vegetables, flowers and a wide array of fresh produce and foodstuffs for the people of Barcelona. Space for a market was lacking inside the city walls due to the narrowness of the streets and squares. The first permanent market in the area was designed in 1840. It was built on land that had been freed up with the demolition of the former convent of Sant Josep – hence its official name.

The wrought-iron structure that still covers the market went up in 1914. It is made from five identical sections, without walls or metal enclosures around its perimeter. The *modernista* arch that presides over the main entrance dates from the same period. It is also made of wrought iron and is surmounted by stained-glass panels set into cement columns covered in *trencadís*, a mosaic technique using broken tile shards that had been invented a few years earlier by Antoni Gaudí.

Palau Güell

Opening times

From Tuesday to Sunday, 10 a.m. to 5.30 p.m., October to March, and 10 a.m. to 8 p.m., April to September.
Closed Mondays, except holidays.
Price: 10€; 8€ students, under 25s, over 65s and unemployed

Born in 1846, Eusebi Güell is one of the leading exemplars of the entrepreneurs who gave impetus to Catalan industry during the second half of the 19th century, fostering a trend that had a notable influence on the culture, politics and society of the region.

Impressed by the designs of the young Antoni Gaudí, Güell soon signed up the brilliant architect to refurbish his summer residence in the district of Les Corts de Sarrià and 1885 he had no hesitation in entrusting him with the design of his new town house, just off La Rambla, in the centre of Barcelona old town.

At the time, all the eminent Barcelona families were moving to the new Eixample district that had been laid out just 30 years earlier by Ildefons Cerdà and was equipped with all the modern conveniences that were lacking in the narrow streets of the old town. However, Güell remained committed to La Rambla and El Raval, a neighbourhood whose social and sanitary conditions had notably declined due to the overcrowding caused by the massive influx of people

Palau Güell

from the rest of Spain who had come here in search of work.

This is why the businessman and patron of the arts suggested that Gaudí design a townhouse that would face inwards, with an austere façade and a luxurious interior, set out around a central lobby with vertical proportions that ran from the ground floor to the top of the building, surmounted by a parabolic dome pierced by a large central lantern surrounded by small perforations resembling stars.

The inward-facing architecture of the building enabled Güell to isolate himself from the bustling atmosphere of Carrer Nou de Rambla and to organise concerts, literary gatherings and cultural encounters in the rooms of his residence while, outside, the working classes sought entertainment in much more mundane pursuits.

The façade of the Palau Güell is extremely contained in comparison with most of Gaudí's works. Güell is said to have made predominant use of grey calcareous stone on the façade, arranged in rectilinear forms and almost devoid of decorative elements, in order to convey the values of Christianity, with deliberate austerity, to the decadent Barcelona of the end of the 19th century.

Inside, the building looks like a sumptuous townhouse, with marble the main material used as a wall and floor covering. The ground floor was designed to allow carriages to enter and leave the building – the coach house in the basement is one of Gaudí's most thought-provoking spaces –; the first floor was for entertaining guests; the Güell family lived on the mezzanine floor; and the servants lived on the top floor which was covered by a flat roof where Gaudí eschewed the overall sobriety of the project and designed 20 chimneys that are clad in the widest variety of colours and textures.

Museu d'Art Contemporani de Barcelona MACBA

Opening times
Tuesday, except public holidays: closed.
Winter (25th September to 23rd June): Monday, Wednesday, Thursday and Friday: 11am-8pm; Saturday: 10am-8pm; Sunday and public holidays: 10am-3pm
Summer (24th June to 24th September): Monday and Wednesday: 11am-8pm; Thursday and Friday: 11am-midnight; Saturday: 10am-8pm; Sunday and public holidays: 10am-3pm
Prices: 7.50 €; students and groups of 20 people upwards: 6 €; over 65s, unemployed and under 14s, free

Since the 1950s, Barcelona had aspired to having its own museum of contemporary art that would showcase works by the most prestigious Catalan artists of the post-Civil War period. In 1995, after years of effort and changes in fortune, this wish became a reality with the opening of the Museu d'Art Contemporani de Barcelona (MACBA), a

Museu d'Art Contemporani de Barcelona MACBA

Barcelona +info

major cultural facility built on the site of the old poorhouse, the Casa de la Caritat.

The prestigious American architect Richard Meier secured the brief to create this elongated building, with a main façade that is 120 metres long. The predominant straight lines contrast with a circular volume that covers four floors and connects the different galleries.

The winner of the Pritzker Prize (which is often referred to as the Nobel Prize for Architecture) in 1984, Meier is a rationalist architect who is strongly influenced by Le Corbusier and whose main concern is to ensure natural light floods into every corner of the building he is designing. With its huge windows and skylights, the Macba is no exception. Even the galleries on the ground floor let in natural light from above as a result of the system devised by Meier, who asked for some of the ironwork to be removed from the line of the façade to allow light to filter into this space.

The Macba shares another of the essential traits of Meier's buildings: its white cladding. White is the architect's favourite colour due to its purity, reflective properties and changing tonalities throughout the day.

The collection on display in the museum's galleries gives us a clear idea of the artistic trends that emerged during the 20th century, particularly over recent decades, although it tends to avoid exhibiting works in purely chronological order.

As you would expect, Catalan art is widely represented, with works by Joan Brossa, Antoni Clavé, Antoni Tàpies, Modest Cuixart, Josep Guinovart, Josep Maria de Sucre, Antoni Vila Arrufat, Albert Ràfols Casamada and Joan Miró, and many more besides. Contemporary Spanish artists featured include Miquel Barceló, Eduardo Chillida and Jorge Oteiza, and the international art scene is represented by artists as diverse as Alexander Calder, Marcel Duchamp, Brassaï, Jean-Michel Basquiat and John Cage.

Seafront

Reials Drassanes Museu Marítim

Opening times
Monday to Sunday: 10am-8pm. Annual closing 25th and 26th December and 1st and 6th January.
Prices: 2.50 €; visitors aged 7 to 16, over 65s, students under 25, 1.25 €; Sunday from 3pm and under 7s: free.
The permanent exhibition at the Museu Marítim will be closed due to the restoration of the Drassanes and the refurbishment of the museum. Opening planned in 2012.

The Reials Drassanes, the best-preserved medieval shipyards in the world, stand at the point where La

Rambla meets the harbour waters. They were begun in the 13th-century and constructed in several phases using a highly functional and rational building method.

In 1255, Pere the Great, the King of Aragon, warned that Barcelona's original shipyards were becoming obsolete and ordered the building of a new shipbuilding complex in the south of the city, outside the city walls. Initially, the building was a simple courtyard surrounded by porticoed walls and with turrets at each corner. However, a century later, in 1378, the entire surface area of the shipyards was covered over by eight parallel vaulted naves underpinned by broad square arches and clad in wood.

This functional, understated and spacious layout made it possible to build up to 30 galleys simultaneously. This capacity was pivotal in making the Crown of Aragon one of the Mediterranean's main military and trading powers, as most of the ships in the Catalan-Aragon fleet were built here.

At the beginning of the 17th century, the Catalan government decided to add three new naves to the wing closest to La Rambla and adhered strictly to the design of the medieval building. In the 18th century, the two central naves were joined together to form a higher single nave. This structure survives today.

During this period, the Drassanes came under the ownership of the Spanish army and a defensive wall was built around them. The shipyards were used for another purpose: first as a barracks and then as a weapons arsenal. By the mid-19th century the army had left and the Drassanes were restored. Since 1941, they have been home to the Museu Marítim, a cultural facility with a permanent exhibition that hosts temporary exhibitions to disseminate every aspect of seafaring life and show the close historic relationship between the city and the marine environment.

Museu d'Història de Catalunya MHC

Opening times
Tuesday to Saturday: 10am-7pm; Wednesday: 10am-8pm; Sunday and public holidays: 10am-2.30pm; Mondays, except public holidays: closed.
Prices: 4 € permanent exhibition and 3 € temporary exhibitions; 5 € combined ticket; reduced admission for senior citizens and children and young people aged between 7 and 18; free for over 65s and under 7s

The Palau de Mar is a huge building, larger than a football pitch (it covers a surface area of 1 hectare). Built in 1881, it was initially used as the General Trade Warehouses to store the goods that were unloaded at Barcelona harbour. Since 1996, it has been home to the Museu d'Història de Catalunya, a cultural complex designed to disseminate historic events in Catalonia.

Barcelona +info

The warehouses are one of the few surviving buildings from Barcelona's old port and are among the most highly prized architectural ensembles from Catalonia's rich industrial heritage. They were built to store the goods that were not intended for domestic consumption and were loaded back onto other ships to continue their journey to their final destination. With this aim in mind, the engineer Maurici Garrán designed a spacious, innovative building with outer walls made of brick and a flat roof – the best insulation to protect goods from the bad weather and fire – and an inner framework of laminated steel, which was extremely effective when an open-plan space that could withstand heavy loads was required.

In Barcelona at the time, the harbour area was known as the docks and the General Trade Warehouses were inspired by the English dockland architecture of the period. However, as they had been built some distance away from the harbour mouth, they were seldom used for their intended purpose. The building was put to a number of uses, and was eventually restored for the Olympic Games and converted into the headquarters of the Museu d'Història de Catalunya. The museum's permanent exhibition tells of the historic events and everyday life in Catalonia at different periods, from the Lower Palaeolithic to the present day: its roots, the birth of the nation, the conquest of the Mediterranean, its location on the edge of the Spanish Empire, industrialisation, the recovery of national identity, Franco's repression and subsequent reinstatement of devolved government bodies.

L'Aquàrium Barcelona

Opening times
Open every day of the year.
From Monday to Friday: 9.30 a.m. to 9 p.m.
Weekends and official holidays: 9.30 a.m. to 9.30 p.m.
July and August: 9.30 a.m. to 11 p.m.
Prices: adults: 17.75€; 4 to 12 years old: 12.75€; over 60: 14.75€

Located in the Port of Barcelona, the Aquarium is one of the biggest sea life centres in the world, with a total of around 11,000 examples of 450 distinct species. While it faithfully reproduces all the ocean environments on the planet, including spectacular coral reefs, the Aquarium specialises in the Mediterranean ecosystems, which occupy 21 of the 35 marine exhibits which are housed there. The largest of all is the monumental Oceanarium, with the main attraction being the numerous sharks which can be seen from the glass underwater tunnel, 80 metres long. Also of note is the exhibition with small aquariums, called Planeta Aqua. This is where you can find many of the small creatures which have adapted to the very diverse and extreme aquatic conditions which exist: glacial temperatures, the

L'Aquàrium Barcelona

Frank Gehry's *Fish*

obscurity of the deep sea abyss, warm tropical waters… And you can also discover the importance of the Earth's seas in the development of our planet over more than 3,500 million years. A very important zone for families with children is ¡Explora!, an interactive space, both educational and enjoyable in character. Conceived so that children can find out more about the marine world, it has more than 50 interactive games to touch, look at, listen to, investigate and discover nature.

Frank Gehry's *Fish*

During building work on the Olympic Village for the 1992 Games, the American Frank Gehry, one of the world's most in-demand architects, was commissioned to design a sculptural structure that was to be placed at the foot of the skyscrapers in the Olympic Marina. The designer of the prestigious Guggenheim Museum in Bilbao, Gehry is the standard bearer of deconstructivism and introduces organic forms drawn from nature into his architecture, so that many of the buildings he designs, modelled on eye-catching curves, end up resembling vast sculptures.

This is why it is only natural that the design of sculptural figures is one of his passions. Indeed, the evocative, tapering form of the fish, with its glimmering scales, had captured his imagination as an art object since childhood. It therefore comes as no surprise that fish are a main

feature in Gehry's work, such as the Fishdance Restaurant in Kobe (Japan) and the Goldfish in the Olympic Marina, a vast structure made from interwoven steel strips that reflect the copper and golden tones of the sun.

Museu Blau MCNB

Opening times
Winter (1 October to 31 May):
Tuesday to Friday: 10 a.m. to 7 p.m.
Saturdays and Sundays: 10 a.m. to 8 p.m.
Summer (1 June to 30 September):
Tuesday to Sunday: 10 a.m. to 9 p.m.
Closed Mondays, except official holidays, and on 25 December and 1 January.
Entrance free on the first Sunday of each month, and after 3 p.m. every Sunday.
Prices: 7€ (Museu Blau and the Montjuïc Botanic Gardens). Concessions: 5€

The Museu Blau is the resplendent centre for the Barcelona Museum of Natural Sciences. It opened in 2011, in the Forum Building, the principal enclave for the 2004 Forum of Cultures in Barcelona. The "Blue Museum" was a project by the prestigious studio of Swiss architects, Herzog & de Meuron, authors of, among other buildings, the Beijing National Stadium, the Allianz Arena football stadium in Munich and the extension of the Tate Modern in London, as well as adapting the Forum Building for its final use for exhibitions.

With an immense floor area in the form of an equilateral triangular, 180 metres

Barcelona +info

on each side and 25 metres high, the Forum Building has a surface of 9,000 square metres with vast potential as a museum. Planeta Vida (Planet Life) is the name of the permanent reference exhibition at the Museu Blau. This uses the best contemporary criteria to exhibit the 4,500 most representative pieces from the more than three million which were in the collection of the former Geology, Zoology and Botany city museums. These city museums opened in the 19th century to give people the opportunity to discover the natural heritage of Catalonia, the Mediterranean and other regions of the world. The other displays all worthy of note are: La biografía de la Tierra – a journey through the history of life on Earth; Los laboratorios de la vida – a series of small exhibitions on specific themes related to Biology; temporary exhibitions and Niu de Ciència, a zone created to awaken scientific curiosity in children, suitable for children up to six years old.

L'Eixample + Gràcia

Basilica of the Sagrada Família

Opening times
October to March: 9am-6pm; April to September: 9am-8pm; 25th and 26th December and 1st and 6th January: 9am-2pm.

Prices: 12,50 €; guided or audioguided tour: 16,50 €; senior citizens and under 18s: 10,50 €; under 10s and disabled, free. The price doesn't include a visit to the top of the towers. The ride in the lift costs 2.50 €.

Guided tours
English: May to October, 11am, 1pm, 3pm, 5pm; November to April: 11am, 1pm
Catalan: Sunday 12 noon
Spanish: May to October, 12 noon and 4pm; November to April, 12 noon

The Sagrada Família is one of the iconic symbols of Barcelona and one of the most famous churches in the world. This is partly because of its unique architecture, created by the genius Antoni Gaudí, and partly because its construction process has mirrored the age of the great cathedrals, when it took two centuries to build a great Gothic church. The first stone of the church was laid in 1882 and Gaudí, its originator, died in 1926, but the Sagrada Família is still under construction more than a decade into the 21st century.

The genius of *modernista* architecture devoted 43 years of his professional life to supervising work on the church, from the age of 31 to a few days before his death. He put all his technical and artistic know-how into the building. This prompted him to say that nature was the greatest inspiration for his work and that by observing it he drew the necessary elements to create the structures and decorative features that make his buildings so unique.

Basilica of the Sagrada Família

Curiously enough, Gaudí wasn't the first architect to work on the Sagrada Família. The church, which was an initiative of a devout Barcelona book-seller, was originally designed in the neo-Gothic style by Francesc de Paula del Villar, who was the official architect of the bishopric at the time. Nevertheless, the differences in criteria between Villar and the developer made it possible for the young Gaudí – a very promising artist who had barely completed two projects – to take over the venture a year after it had begun, when only part of the crypt and apse had been built.

To avoid wasting the money that had already been invested, Gaudí didn't discard what had been built, but he had no hesitation in changing the project completely, making it much more ambitious. Technically, the archi-ect developed a revolutionary struc-ure, that is robust yet light and could ale extraordinary heights without the clusion of buttresses. The highest int of the central nave is 45 metres, e existing towers stand 125 metres gh and, when it is built, the dome will tand 170 metres high.

Symbolically, Gaudí became a true expert in the Catholic liturgy, so that he could adapt the church to all the require-ments of worship. Throughout the years, the huge vertical and horizontal spaces inside the building that occupies an entire block in the Eixample were transformed into a true Bible in stone, with sculptural references to countless Biblical passages and characters.

The north-east-facing Nativity façade may be Gaudí's greatest legacy. During the last few years of his life, the great architect focused all his energy on ensuring the project for the symbolic elements on this façade was well under way, to provide his successors with clear pointers to his decorative ideas for the entire church. The façade depicts the main events in the birth, childhood and adolescence of Christ with sculptural groups replete with dynamism and warmth that depict well-known scenes from the New Testament, such as the Annunciation, the Adoration of the Magi, the flight into Egypt, the Massacre of the Innocents and the Presentation in the Temple.

At the time of Gaudí's death, only the crypt, apse, part of the cloister and the Nativity façade had been completed, and the four remaining towers were nearing completion. However, the archi-tect's death, the financial problems encountered by the developers, and the outbreak of the Spanish Civil War ten years later, brought work to a standstill. Building recommenced in 1954 with the Passion façade.

Gaudí's original plans and sketches were destroyed in an arson attack dur-ing the Civil War, but they showed a church with five naves and a transept, a unique cloister in the style of a deam-bulatory that encompasses almost the entire building, three monumental facades with porticos and 18 towers: 12 bell towers dedicated to the apostles,

61 **Basilica of the Sagrada Família**

Barcelona +info

four towers dedicated to the evangelists, one dedicated to the Virgin Mary, and the tallest, dedicated to Christ, that will eventually surmount the dome, making the Sagrada Família the city's tallest building.

Only eight of the 18 towers have been completed: those on the Nativity and Passion façades. The symbolic elements on the latter, by the sculptor Josep Maria Subirachs, contrast sharply with the vitality and innocence of the opposite façade, as it depicts the suffering and death of Jesus Christ using angular, hieratic figures, in a tableau devoid of ornamentation, as Gaudí had intended in his original sketches.

The interior of the church once again proves Gaudí's creative genius. In order to cover over a space for 14,000 worshippers and a choir of 1,200 singers, the Catalan architect once again drew inspiration from nature to create the tree-like column that branches out to a great height to underpin a series of curious vaults in the shape of palm leaves with lanterns that allow natural light into the building. Gaudí envisaged four types of columns designed according to the weight they had to bear: the lightest – 1.05 metres in diameter – are made from sandstone; the ones measuring 1.40 are granite; and the ones measuring 1.75, are basalt, while the four columns that bear the most weight, located at the intersection of the central nave and transept, are 2.10 metres in diameter and made of porphyry, an extremely resistant igneous rock.

Just a few metres away from this grand and sumptuous décor, next to the Passion façade, a simple, single-storey brick building attracts the attention of visitors. It is the Sagrada Família school which was designed by Gaudí to educate the children of the neighbourhood – at the time, a working-class district – and the children of the masons who were working on the church. At first sight, the building looks simple, although the undulating shape of its roof and its walls conceal a boldness that amazed the father of rationalism, the Swiss architect Le Corbusier, when he visited Barcelona in 1928.

Casa Milà "La Pedrera"

Opening times
November to February: Monday to Sunday: 9am-6.30pm; March to October: Monday to Sunday: 9am-8pm. Yearly closing: 25th and 26th December, 1st January and 6th to 14th January. Prices: 14 €; students and unwaged, 10 €; under 13s, admission free; audioguide available: 4 €
Guided tours
For schools only, weekdays: 10am, 12 noon and 3pm

In 1906, Antoni Gaudí had already gained great popularity in Barcelona as the architect of the Sagrada Família and the designer of the homes of some of the most powerful industrialists of

Casa Milà "La Pedrera"

the time. One of these, the Casa Calvet, on Barcelona's Carrer Casp, had won a prize from the city council as the best building of 1900. Five years later, another of Gaudí's works, the full-scale refurbishment of the Casa Batlló, won the admiration of experts and laypeople because of its boldness and creativity.

One of the new admirers of Gaudí's style was the property developer Pere Milà, whose father was one of Batlló's business partners. Milà was recently married and he decided to commission Gaudí to build his new home on the corner of Passeig de Gràcia and Carrer de Provença. As was customary at the time, the developer was to live on the first floor and the upper floors would be put up for sale or rent.

Gaudí was at the height of his creative powers and he designed his most personal residential building, which was met with incredulity by the owners of the building – who he eventually fell out with – and Barcelona society as a whole, who nicknamed the building *pedrera* (the Catalan for quarry) due to the naturalistic forms of its façade, a true architectural sculpture in undulating stone that contrasts with the audacious tangle of wrought iron that makes up the railings of the balconies and terraces.

Today, opinions have changed and La Pedrera is considered one of Gaudí's major landmarks. When the architect began working on the design for the Casa Milà he was so sure of his structural and aesthetic approach that he allowed himself to relinquish traditional building methods and to investigate as-yet-unexplored technical and artistic paths. The result of this journey, La Pedrera, is a building of a boldness that was deemed inappropriate at the time.

On a vast corner site, Gaudí was courageous enough to design a large, six-storey building with a basement and attic space based on a revolutionary structure of pillars and cast-iron girders which allowed him to dispense with load-bearing walls. This enabled him to tailor the interior layout of every flat to the needs of their occupants, and made him the forerunner of the concept of the open-plan floor adopted by the rationalists two decades later.

In order to reinforce this ideal combination of resistance and lightness, the architect designed a free-standing façade which is a self-supporting structure, separate from the rest of the building, to which it is attached by small girders set into the blocks of stone.

Another innovation that Gaudí had saved for the Casa Milà was the inclusion of one of the first car parks in Spain in the basement. This meant that he had to design a spacious lobby that would be big enough to allow vehicles to manoeuvre freely. Gaudí finally created a double lobby with one entrance from the corner and another from Carrer de Provença, to make it easier for cars to circulate.

This double lobby utilised the open space left by the two interior courtyards,

Casa Milà "La Pedrera"

which were designed to let the maximum natural light into the inner areas of the building, some of which were some distance away from the façade. Light was so important to Gaudí that he decided to dispense with the monumental staircase leading to the upper floors to avoid blocking out light in the courtyards, which were transformed into interior façades. The architect had two lifts fitted instead. These were seen as a great novelty at the time. Gaudí designed three stairwells in less visible areas which were connected to the service areas on each floor.

The first floor, which was reserved in its entirety for the Milà family, covers a surface area of 1,300 square metres, the equivalent of ten large apartments in the neighbourhood. It has 35 rooms, including living rooms, bathrooms, kitchens and servants' quarters, and is the only floor that is accessible from the lobbies by two flights of steps designed for the sole use of the Milà family. On the upper storeys, every floor is divided into three or four dwellings, all of them with their main façade, rear façade and inner courtyard.

This large amount of available space enabled Gaudí to devise an extensive decorative programme. The Catalan architect put his great creativity and the professional skills of his associates to the test in order to endow the building with countless ornamental details that involved painters, sculptors, plasterers, ceramicists, cabinetmakers, metalworkers and glassworkers. Among all these contributions from artists and artisans, the hexagonal tile with its marine motifs that Gaudí designed for the games room on the first floor is particularly memorable. It was later transformed into the paving stones on the Passeig de Gràcia and has since become a symbol of Barcelona.

In contrast with this ornamental richness, the attic space is pure architecture. Gaudí designed it to house the heating and cooling systems to protect the rest of the building from the rigours of winter and summer, and the laundry, where clothes were washed and dried. The attic is an open-plan space with 270 catenary arches – the parabolic construction Gaudí introduced to the world of building – made entirely of brick.

Unadorned and evocative, this structure underpins the rooftop, an area that cannot be seen from the street and is seldom considered by architects, which Gaudí transformed into a dreamlike landscape, bursting with a variety of forms, textures and lustres.

Park Güell

Opening times
365 days a year:
November to February, 10 a.m. to 6 p.m.;
March and October, 10 a.m. to 7 p.m.;
April and September, 10 a.m. to 8 p.m.;
May and August, 10 a.m. to 9 p.m.
Admission free

In the years spanning the end of the 19th and the beginning of the 20th centuries, Barcelona was in the throes of a building boom. The development of the Eixample on the broad unpopulated plain multiplied the surface area of the city which spread to the boundaries of the small neighbouring towns and villages and eventually absorbed them.

Some businessmen saw the great business potential of this property boom. Among them was the industrialist Eusebi Güell, the friend and patron of Antoni Gaudí, who had discovered the concept of the garden city on his trips to England. This urban-planning movement sought to bring together the best of rural and city life in a single area.

In 1900, Güell sought Gaudí's help in designing a garden city on land in the north of Barcelona. The development was called Park Güell, and the industrialist wanted to give it symbolic value that would hark back to Christian values and Catalan traditions as a way of combating the alienation of the new industrial society.

Gaudí took charge of the design of the communal areas of the park, from the gatehouses to the Calvary at the highest point of the park, as well as the marketplace, the monumental staircase, the plaza and network of paths. Completely enclosed by a security wall, the park originally had 60 triangular plots where each property owner could build their house according to basic building standards.

Gaudí was faced with a huge amount of building work so he chose to design prefabricated-concrete modules in different shapes and for different uses. By covering them in *trencadís* – ceramic shards – in a variety of colours and textures, the architect managed to keep building moving along at an efficient pace, without giving onlookers the impression that Park Güell was a "mass-produced" project.

The administrative offices and the

caretaker's lodge stand on either side of the main gate, their dreamlike forms marking the boundary between the sombre city and a development bursting with happiness and colour.

In his application of the symbolic elements suggested by Güell, Gaudí approached the ascent from the gate-houses to the summit of the park as a path of Christian purification. The flight of steps that connects the entrance with the marketplace is the first section of this path. Here you will find the park's best-known feature: the dragon clad in colourful *trencadís* mosaic.

The marketplace was designed so that the residents wouldn't have to leave the estate to look for provisions, and is inspired by the temples of Ancient Greece. Its vaulted ceiling features one of the jewels of the park: the ceramic soffits depicting the sun and moon designed by the architect and artist Josep Maria Jujol, who was a follower and associate of Gaudí's.

The Doric columns in the marketplace underpin the vast plaza, a sandy espla-nade designed as a meeting place for the residents. A curving cement bench encloses the entire plaza providing a place to sit as well as a balcony and viewing point over the city. The bench is more than 100 metres long and is entirely covered in *trencadís* mosaic; it was designed – like the soffits in the marketplace – by Jujol, and can be considered one of the first abstract artworks.

For Gaudí, one of the greatest chal-lenges of the park was the design of its network of paths as it went beyond the parameters of architecture to embrace the field of town planning. The steeply sloping terrain of the hill-side where the park was built made it necessary for the architect to design a series of viaducts supported by sloping columns. To give a natural appearance to the ensemble, Gaudí had these struc-tures clad in unhewn limestone quarried on the site.

In spite of the undisputed brilliance of these structural and decorative solutions, the Park Güell development project was a failure. In 1914, with all the communal areas completed, only 60 of the plots had been sold. This led Güell to bring building work to a halt. In 1922, the city council purchased the complex and turned it into a public park, which in recent decades has become one of Barcelona's main tourist attrac-tions, a status consolidated in 1984 when it was declared a Unesco World Heritage Site.

Casa Batlló

Opening times
Every day of the year, 9am-8pm
Admission: 18.15 €
Audioguide available

With the development of the Eixample district, the wide, central Passeig de Gràcia became the avenue of choice for wealthy Barcelona families. The

industrialists who had made their fortunes during decades of feverish economic activity competed with one another to commission the top architects of the day and build the most luxurious, comfortable houses along this boulevard.

The finest example of this rivalry is the so-called "block of discord", on the western side of the Passeig de Gràcia between Carrer Consell de Cent and Carrer Aragó. Stretching for just over 100 metres, it is the site of the Casa Lleó Morera, designed by Lluís Domènech i Montaner, the creator of the Palau de la Música; the Casa Mulleras, by Enric Sagnier Villavecchia, who designed the church at the top of Tibidabo; the Casa Amatller, by Josep Puig i Cadafalch, who designed the Casa de les Punxes; and the Casa Batlló, by Antoni Gaudí, which was begun in 1904.

The commission was particularly unusual for the mastermind behind the Sagrada Família, as a building with sober architectural lines that had been built 29 years earlier already stood on the site purchased by the industrialist Josep Batlló. Batlló suggested demolishing the house, but the architect persuaded him to preserve and refurbish it, adding an extra storey and attic, and radically altering its exterior and interior.

In spite of having to adhere to a pre-existing structure, at the time Gaudí was at the height of his creative powers and imbued the building with all his artistic personality, to the extent that the Casa Batlló and Park Güell are considered to be the buildings which saw him completely dispense with the influences of historic styles – Gothic, Moorish, baroque...– and begin to apply his own artistic convictions, in all their purity, based on the shapes he observed in nature.

In his endeavours to make the building taller, Gaudí came up against the restrictions of municipal guidelines. In order to safeguard his project and comply with the law, the architect designed a curved roof with rhomboid tiles that resemble the scales of a dragon, and created a terrace on the corner with the neighbouring Casa Amatller, so that passers-by would be able to see the continuity between the two buildings from the Passeig de Gràcia.

Although Gaudí preserved the original layout and size of the windows, he clad the original walls in stone, ceramic and glass, making the façade of the Casa Batlló one of the main attractions of the Passeig de Gràcia, capturing the attention of passers-by, in spite of the spectacular neighbouring buildings.

The first-floor gallery and balconies, carved in stone with curious organic shapes that look like bones, dominate the lower half of the façade, while on the upper half, small glazed ceramic shards gleam in the sunlight on a slightly undulating surface, creating a similar effect to viewing an impressionist painting.

Gaudí saved the most important structural renovations for the light well,

Casa Batlló

by widening it considerably in order to allow in more light and improve ventilation, without sacrificing space for the staircase used by the other residents in the block. Moreover, in order to make the most of overhead light, the architect had the entire light well clad in highly reflective tiles and covered the small indoor terraces of the ground-floor flats in glass tiles.

Inside the building, the two most unusual spaces are the first-floor flat, designed as the owner's residence, and the attic. Both are fine examples of the naturalism that imbued Gaudí's work at the peak of his career. On the mezzanine floor, this trend is seen particularly on a decorative level, due to the cladding on the walls, whereas in the attic, Gaudí's preference for organic forms is shown in the structure of the space, as the succession of catenary arches gives visitors the impression that they are inside the thoracic cavity of a large animal.

Casa Amatller

Guided tours
Monday to Friday morning or Tuesday and Thursday afternoons, for pre-booked groups; Friday at 12 noon (English) and Wednesday at 12 noon (Catalan and Spanish) for individual visitors, as well as pre-booked visitors. Admission: 10 € individual visit, 8 € group visit.

Like the Casa Batlló next door, the Casa Amatller – which is one of the most unusual buildings on the "block of discord" – was built around an existing building of scant architectural interest. In 1898, the chocolate manufacturer Antoni Amatller commissioned the *modernista* architect Josep Puig i Cadalfach to carry out a complete refit of the building. Puig i Cadalfach had already designed the Casa de les Punxes, among other buildings.

Following the historicist lines that defined much Catalan art-nouveau architecture, Puig i Cadalfach designed a neo-Gothic townhouse that combined home-grown elements with the characteristic features of the Flemish Gothic style, such as the stepped gable that surmounts the façade.

Puig designed a building with a lower floor, four storeys and an attic, with a pitched roof that was hidden behind the gable. The façade is divided into three strips: the frontage on the ground floor is made entirely of stone and has three doorways of different heights with ogee arches; the central strip is covered with *sgraffito* work and has a wide wrought-iron balcony and a gallery at the side with Flamboyant decorations on the mezzanine. The gable is clad in multi-coloured ceramic tiles, which glimmer in the light in contrast with the opacity of the rest of the façade.

The first floor, which was solely used as the home of the Amatller family and was set out around a broad light well, features a plethora of sculptural ele-

Casa Amatller

Barcelona +info

ments, stained-glass windows, ceramic dados that are Moorish in inspiration and a Roman-influenced mosaic floor with black and white motifs. The furnishings were also designed by Puig i Cadafalch.

Fundació Antoni Tàpies

Opening times
Tuesday to Sunday: 10am-7pm.
Monday closed.
Prices: 7 €; students and senior citizens, 5.60 €
Guided tours
Phone bookings: T 93 207 58 62
e-mail bookings: reserves@ftapies.com

In 1984, during his search for permanent premises to house a museum for his works, the Catalan painter and sculptor Antoni Tàpies visited the building that had once been home to the publishing house Montaner i Simon, in the heart of the Eixample district. Although in a state of neglect, following its closure, Tàpies realised that the building was the ideal site for his foundation.

Montaner i Simon was one of Spain's leading publishers during the late 19th and early 20th centuries. In 1882 they moved to a building in the Eixample with a basement, ground floor and three storeys that had been designed by the young architect Lluís Domènech i Montaner, the nephew of one of the owners who, years later, was to design the Palau de la Música and Hospital de Sant Pau.

The Montaner i Simon building was a pioneer in many aspects: along with Gaudí's Casa Vicens it was Barcelona's first *modernista* building, and it was the first city-centre building to have an exposed brick façade and a wrought-iron structure. The use of these materials, closely associated with the industrialisation process, reflect the use of the building for manufacturing, although Domènech i Montaner imbued it with a number of structural and ornamental features characteristic of a town house.

The façade combines classical-style decorative elements with Moorish-inspired details and is surmounted by Tàpies' sculpture *Cloud and Chair* which was made to tie in with the opening of the museum, in 1990. Made from anodised aluminium tubing and stainless-steel mesh, it enhances the height of the building that stands between two taller blocks, and highlights its new function as a museum.

The museum hosts temporary exhibitions and is also a showcase for more than 300 works by Tàpies, the standard-bearer of informalism and one of the most renowned exponents of contemporary Spanish art. In the basement – which once housed the publishing house presses – you can see the artist's private collection, with works by Goya, Zurbarán, Picasso, Miró, Georges Braque, Hans Arp, Paul Klee and Wassily Kandinsky, among others.

Fundació Antoni Tàpies

Hospital de la Santa Creu i Sant Pau

Guided tours
See opening times at www.santpau.es

The Hospital de la Santa Creu was founded in 1401 in the Raval district and was the city's main hospital for more than 400 years. The breakthroughs made in healthcare and hygiene during the 19th century led the medical and municipal authorities to warn that the Gothic-style building was no longer suitable for treating the sick.

After several decades fraught with controversy, work on a new hospital to replace the old one in the Raval began in 1902. The project was made possible due to donations from Pau Gil i Serra, a Catalan banker living in Paris who gave half of his inheritance to ensure the project came to fruition. The people in charge of the new hospital appended the Saint's name of the patron to the hospital as a tribute to his generous donation. In just a few years time, it came to be known as the Hospital de Sant Pau.

The project was awarded to the great *modernista* architect Lluís Domènech i Montaner, who was commissioned to design the Palau de la Música a few years later. A large plot of land on the northern edge of the Eixample was purchased to house the hospital covering a surface area equivalent to nine blocks: a vast area that made it possible to build the largest civil ensemble of the *modernista* era in Catalonia, with 27 pavilions as well as the administrative buildings and other services.

However, by 1911, Gil i Serra's donation had been used up, bringing building work to a halt. The main building and nine medical pavilions had been completed. Building work recommenced three years later under the supervision of Domènech i Montaner's son Pere Domènech i Roura. He oversaw the building of four more pavilions, adhering faithfully to the *modernista* canons stipulated by his father, in spite of the fact that the aesthetic movement was considered somewhat dated. Domènech i Roura designed the last buildings in the complex in a baroque-influenced monumentalist style in the late 1920s. The notable differences in style compared with those of his predecessor can be seen in the hospital church and the convalescent home.

In his original design, Domènech i Montaner presented an integrated project that brought together architecture and town planning and took on board some of the key ideas behind the utopian theory of garden cities. Indeed, the hospital consists of a series of individual pavilions, separated by broad landscaped areas and connected by underground passageways that let in light from above. Strangely enough, the complex is set out on diagonal lines, in contrast with the grid system of the Eixample, breaking the discipline stipulated by the town planner Ildefons

Hospital de la Santa Creu i Sant Pau

Barcelona +info

Cerdà, whose postulates were never to the liking of Domènech i Montaner.

Most of the buildings are made from exposed brick and feature a whole host of sculptural decorative elements in ceramic and mosaic, largely inspired by Gothic and Moorish art. The administrative block, at the northern end of the Avinguda de Gaudí, gives passers-by wonderful and unique views as a result of the diagonal arrangement and the pointed spire of the clock tower which is inspired by Nordic architecture.

The pavilions are set out in a regular pattern at a distance from one another and consist of a large open-plan room without any architectural divisions and roofs underpinned by eight pointed arches. There are additional rooms on either side of the open-plan room. Outside the building, Domènech i Montaner chose to break up the square lines of the pavilions by placing circular turrets at the corners.

Sants + Montjuïc

Museu Nacional d'Art de Catalunya MNAC

Opening times
Tuesday to Saturday: 10am-7pm
Sundays and public holidays: 10am-2.30pm. Closed Monday except public holidays. Yearly closing: 1st January, 1st May and 25th December
Prices: 8.50 € (valid for two days during a month from date of purchase); free for under 16s and over 65s, and for the general public on the first Sunday every month

In 1919, an American art dealer and antiquarian set out on an expedition of the Pyrenees to buy Romanesque murals with a view to selling them on to museums in the United States. They hired the services of the Stefanoni family, a dynasty of restorers who were masters of the *strappo* technique, which made it possible to detach frescoes from the wall and move them without any damage.

The photographer on the expedition alerted the Museum Trust, which supervises art exhibitions in Catalonia, and they purchased all the frescoes and commissioned the Stefanonis to remove them. The Stefanonis visited all the counties in the Pyrenees in search of the murals which had been recorded years earlier by a number of experts, including the *modernista* architect Lluís Domènech i Montaner.

The frescoes were placed under the protection of the Museum Trust until the Museu d'Art de Catalunya opened on Montjuïc in 1934, with this collection of outstanding Romanesque paintings as its key attraction. Over the decades, the MNAC has acquired holdings from other periods, from the late Middle Ages to the 20th century, and currently houses the most important collection of Catalan art across the ages.

Museu Nacional d'Art de Catalunya MNAC

The MNAC is housed in the Palau Nacional de Montjuïc, a landmark building which was the headquarters of the 1929 Barcelona International Exhibition. Designed in the historicist eclectic style that was in fashion at the time, the Palau Nacional combines classical Renaissance elements with others inspired by baroque art and styles that were strongly rooted in Catalonia, the rest of Spain and Europe. The central dome is reminiscent of the domes of Saint Peter's in Rome and Saint Paul's cathedral in London, while the towers at the sides are inspired by the Giralda in Seville.

The museum's holdings are exhibited in chronological order. The visit begins with the murals from the Pyrenees, which make up the world's most important collection of Romanesque painting, and continues with a substantial selection of Gothic, Renaissance, baroque and modern paintings and sculptures, with works by Spanish and other world-renowned artists, including Fra Angelico, Tiepolo, El Greco, Velázquez, Zurbarán, Rubens, Goya, Rodin, Sorolla and Picasso, and a broad sample of 19th-century Catalan art, spanning modernisme to the avant-garde, with works by Marià Fortuny, Ramon Casas, Joaquim Vayreda, Isidre Nonell, Santiago Rusiñol, Antoni Gaudí, Josep Llimona, Pablo Gargallo, Salvador Dalí and Julio González. Works on display also include the important bequest of the Catalan politician Francesc Cambó and part of the Thyssen-Bornemisza collection.

Fundació Joan Miró

Opening times
Tuesday to Saturday, 10 a.m. to 7 p.m. October to June, and 10 a.m. to 8 p.m., July to September; Thursdays, 10 a.m. to 9.30 p.m; Sundays and holidays, 10 a.m. to 2.30 p.m. Closed Mondays, except holidays. Price: 9€; concessions 6€.

In 1968, the galleries of the Hospital de la Santa Creu hosted the first major exhibition of works by the Barcelona-born painter and sculptor, Joan Miró, one of the greatest exponents of surrealism. The success of the exhibition led Miró and the organisers to consider the possibility of creating a permanent museum devoted to his work in the city.

Miró entrusted his friend Josep Lluís Sert with the project for the building. Sert was the co-founder of the influential GATCPAC, a group of architects whose aim was to promote rationalist architecture and the work of its key representatives: the Swiss architect Le Corbusier and the Germans Walter Gropius – the founder of the Bauhaus – and Mies van der Rohe.

In order to fill the galleries of the building designed by Sert, the Fundació Joan Miró was set up in 1975, with works donated by the artist, as well as from the collections of Joan Prats – one of the prime movers behind the foundation –, Miró's wife, Pilar Juncosa, whose collection mainly comprised his early works, and other collectors.

Fundació Joan Miró

Barcelona +info

The museum opened that same year on a site on Montjuïc provided by the city council. In accordance with his aesthetic ideas, Sert's building is an example of rationalist architecture. The exhibition space is set out around a central courtyard, a device inspired by the most ancient Mediterranean traditions, while an octagonal tower ties in with medieval Catalan architecture.

All the rooms and galleries inside the museum – which was extended in 1987 and 2001 according to Sert's original criteria – are filled with natural light as the result of the inclusion of huge overhead lanterns in a quarter-cylinder shape and wide panoramic windows that afford views of the city. In order to give all the spaces inside the museum a human scale, Sert used a set of measurements known as a *modulor*, which was devised by Le Corbusier for this purpose.

The wonderful environment created by Sert provides the setting for more than 200 paintings, some 180 sculptures and 8,000 drawings by Miró, as well as other textiles and ceramics by the artist. This broad retrospective of Miró's work is completed by creations by contemporary artists of the calibre of Marcel Duchamp, Max Ernst, Julio González, Fernand Léger, Henry Moore, Antoni Tàpies and Eduardo Chillida.

Mies van der Rohe Pavilion

Opening times
Tuesday to Sunday, 10 a.m. to 8 p.m.; Mondays, 4 p.m. to 8 p.m.
Closed annually 25 December, and 1 and 6 January.
Price: general 4.6€; students 2.5€, under-18s free.

Following the success of 1888 Universal Exhibition, which brought about a large-scale transformation of the area of the city occupied by the military citadel, Barcelona soon embarked on another event that would once again bring it to worldwide attention. The instigator of the idea was the architect and politician Josep Puig i Cadafalch, the co-designer of the project along with his modernista colleagues, including Lluís Domènech i Montaner and Enric Sagnier i Villavecchia. On this occasion, the area under development was Montjuïc Hill, where the Palau Nacional, Magic Fountain, Olympic Stadium, Poble Espanyol, Teatre Grec and the different palaces and halls that later became the permanent headquarters of the trade fair were built.

Curiously enough, none of the buildings became the greatest architectural landmark of the 1929 Exhibition. That accolade went to the German Pavilion, a temporary structure that was demolished just a few weeks after the exhibition closed. This unique building was designed by the rationalist architect

72 Mies van der Rohe Pavilion

Ludwig Mies van der Rohe. Although relatively small in size and built on a site on the edge of the exhibition ground, it nonetheless became one of the most influential buildings of 20th-century architecture.

Despite its importance, the German Pavilion was dismantled in 1930 and the reusable materials sold. Fifty years later, in 1980, the Catalan architect Oriol Bohigas had the idea of rebuilding an exact replica of the pavilion on its original site. Completed in 1986, it stands to the west of the Magic Fountain, across the road from the Casaramona Factory, where its ground-breaking design continues to delight visitors and passers-by.

Built from steel, glass and four types of marble, the German Pavilion marked the beginning of the Modern Movement: a pioneering architectural trend that advocated simple forms, a lack of ornamentation and the use of steel and reinforced concrete as the main building materials. Mies van der Rohe was one of the pioneers of the movement, which came about as a reaction against art nouveau. It represented a break with classic styles and aimed to take architecture back to its original function – to create spaces for living – and to distance it from its simple aesthetic postulates.

A symbol of the democratic ethos of the Weimar Republic – the regime that came to power following the First World War – the pavilion designed by Mies van der Rohe is quite a simple structure, created from a succession of orthogonal planes. It rests on a plinth of travertine marble and has two reflecting pools and a flat roof underpinned by eight cruciform steel columns. The non-load-bearing marble walls are combined with large expanses of glass that foster interaction between the interior and exterior of the building. To complement this essential piece of architecture, Mies van der Rohe designed the Barcelona Chair, which has become a true design icon, and placed the sculpture *Morning*, by the German Georg Kolbe, in the centre of one of the pools.

CaixaForum - Casaramona Factory

Opening times
Monday to Sunday: from 10am to 8pm; Saturday: from 10am. to 10pm; Wednesdays in July and August: from 10am to 11pm
Admission free

The Catalan art-nouveau movement, *modernisme*, reached the pinnacle of its splendour while the region was experiencing a major industrial boom. It was only natural that both activities would come together in interesting industrial *modernista* architecture, of which the Casaramona Factory is one of the finest examples.

After a fire at his yarn and cloth mill on Montjuïc, the textile entrepreneur

Barcelona +info

Casimir Casaramona, who was a pioneer in the introduction of electricity to industrial manufacturing, commissioned the architect Josep Puig i Cadafalch, the designer of the Casa Amatller and the Casa de les Punxes, to plan a new, more modern,safer facility.

In 1911, Puig i Cadafalch designed a major industrial complex on a square floor plan that is a harmonious combination of functionality and aesthetics. Taking inspiration from medieval castles, the complex comprises 11 buildings of different heights and surface areas, built from brick and iron. The units are rectangular, with a flat roof and Catalan vaulting underpinned by cast-iron columns. The arches rest on buttresses that protrude from the outer walls and are surmounted by pinnacles that detract from the horizontal layout of the ensemble. Two towers that were used as water tanks flank the perimeters of the complex.

In spite of the painstaking design and construction, the new factory was only operational for a short period of time. Casaramona died the same year it opened (1913) and the premises were abandoned for good in 1919. Following the Spanish Civil War, the complex was used as a police barracks. In 1963, the bank, La Caixa, purchased the building and decided to restore it and convert it into the headquarters of Caixaforum (2002), a major exhibition centre that stages temporary exhibitions of works from the extensive art collection of La Caixa Foundation.

Palau Sant Jordi

For 150 years, the organisation of major international events has been one of the engines of urban growth in Barcelona: from the 1888 Universal Exhibition to the 1929 International Exhibition, and more recently, the 1992 Olympic Games and the 2004 Forum of Cultures.

Of these four events, the Olympics played the most decisive role in raising the profile of Barcelona around the world as a dynamic, cutting-edge city and brought about the redevelopment of the Poblenou district – where the Olympic Village was located – and Montjuïc, where most of the competitions were held. The most widely admired building on the Olympic hill is certainly the Palau Sant Jordi, the greatest architectural legacy of the great sporting event.

The multipurpose, indoor sporting arena was designed by the Japanese architect Arata Isozaki, and can host a wide variety of sporting events as well as concerts and other entertainments. The Sant Jordi can seat 17,000 and this capacity can easily be expanded to 24,000 as the result of the modular layout of the stands.

This structural flexibility is one of the main assets of the Sant Jordi, and since it opened in 1990, it has hosted clay-tennis tournaments, indoor motorcycle competitions and been a venue for the 2003 World Swimming

Palau Sant Jordi

Championships, when a 50 × 25 m swimming pool was constructed inside the complex.

However, the most eye-catching feature of Isozaki's landmark is the giant roof which has a span of 128 × 106 metres, making it bigger that a football pitch. Made from glazed ceramic tiles and underpinned by a lightweight yet durable web of articulated steel tubing, it was built on the ground and raised into position using a powerful hydraulic system, a process that took ten days to complete. The exterior of the building is organic in shape and has become one of the iconic landmarks in the Montjuïc Olympic Ring. The centre of the roof is studded with semi-spherical skylights and the undulating shape of the skirt section around the perimeter is inspired by the Mediterranean.

22@

Agbar Tower

The French architect Jean Nouvel, the winner of the prestigious Pritzker Prize in 2008, was commissioned to design the Agbar Tower, the office building that has become the brand image of the technology district 22@: a vast industrial site covering a surface area equivalent to 200 football pitches. In the year 2000, the area began to be transformed into a hub for businesses with large R + D departments, as well as universities, research centres, housing and green areas.

The Agbar Tower stands on a plot adjacent to the Plaça de les Glòries – one of the key areas already featured on Ildefons Cerdà's city plan – and is named after its owners, the Barcelona water company, Aigües de Barcelona. The 34-storey tower has four floors below ground level. At 144 metres high, it the city's third tallest building. According to the designer, the unusual elliptical shape of the building is a tribute to the *modernista* architect Antoni Gaudí, who used a very similar shape for his New York hotel project which never came to fruition.

The tower comprises two oval cylinders surmounted by a glass and steel dome. The inner cylinder houses the lifts, stairs and offices, and the outer one, clad in glass and aluminium, includes one of the key features of the skyscraper: more than 4,500 LED devices that generate thought-provoking luminous images on the façade, a spectacular night-time display that is seen to its full potential on public holidays and special occasions.

Residential neighbourhoods

Museu-Monestir de Pedralbes MUHBA

Opening times
April to October: Tuesday to Friday, 10 a.m. to 5 p.m.; Saturdays 10 a.m. to 7 p.m.; Sundays, 10 a.m. to 8 p.m. Novembre to April: Tuesday to Saturday, 10 a.m to 2 p.m.; Sundays, 10 a.m. to 5 p.m. Closed Mondays.
Price: general, 7€; under-25s and over-65s, 5€; under-16s, free.

Located to the west of the former village of Sarrià, the purity and consistency of the Royal Monastery of Pedralbes make it one of the finest surviving examples of the Catalan Gothic style. These virtues are the result of the speed at which it was

Agbar Tower

built – the main building work took scarcely 13 month–, the few alterations it has undergone throughout its seven centuries in existence and, because, during most of its long history, it has been home to a community of nuns from the Order of Saint Clare, who have zealously guarded it and ensured its conservation.

The monastery is a showcase for many works of art and religious furniture. It was founded in 1327 by Queen Elisenda of Montcada, the fourth wife of King Jaume II of Aragon. Following the king's death, Elisenda moved into a palace adjoining the monastery. Her remains lie in a double-sided tomb located between the church and the cloister which is covered by a reclining statue of the queen. On the side viewed from the church by worshippers, the queen is carved in marble and wears a crown and her royal robes. On the side viewed from the cloister – which can only be seen by the nuns – the monastery's founder is sculpted in terracotta and wears a plain Franciscan habit.

The monastery is set out around a monumental three-tier cloister, each side 40 metres long. The first two tiers were built in the 14th century and are underpinned by pointed arches, while the third, which was added in 1412, is a simple structure of architraves, with octagonal columns and a sloping roof.

The main rooms inside the monastery – the chapter house, the abbey, the refectory and many of the nuns'

cells – open onto this large cloister. One of the highlights is the chapel of Saint Michael, which is totally covered in frescoes painted in 1346 by Ferrer Bassa in a style inspired by the brushwork of the Tuscan genius of the *Trecento* Giotto di Bondone.

The church, which occupies an entire wing of the cloister, features the understated decoration and predominant horizontal lines of the Catalan Gothic style. It has a single nave, with seven sections with ogival vaults and side chapels placed between the buttresses.

Outside the monastery building, opposite the square leading into it, stands the *Conventet*, or little convent, which was built in the 14th century to house the friars who provided spiritual guidance for the nuns. The building was restored in 1920 by the *modernista* and *noucentista* architect Enric Sagnier i Villavecchia, who added a tower from the ancient wall that once surrounded the monastery and decorated it with Romanesque elements from the church of Santa Maria in Besalú which had been demolished.

Museu-Monestir de Pedralbes

Camp Nou-
FC Barcelona

Opening times

Museum visit and Camp Nou tour:
Monday to Saturday, 10 a.m. to 6.30
p.m. except 4 April to 9 October, 10 a.m.
to 8 p.m.; Sundays and holidays,
10 a.m. to 2.30 p.m.; 31 December
10 a.m. to 2.30 p.m.
Last Camp Nou tour starts one hour
before museum closes. On match days,
the museum closes three hours early
and there is no tour of the Camp Nou
stadium.
Closed annually 25 December, and
1 and 6 January.
Price: general 19€, under 13s, 15.5€;
under 5s, free.

FC Barcelona, one of Barcelona and
Catalonia's main sources of pride, lived
through a golden age in the 1940s and
50s, due, in part, to the leadership of
the extraordinary Hungarian footballer
Ladislao Kubala, whose amazing skill
was the main reason why the capacity
of the old stadium in Les Corts became
too small. In 1954, building work on a
new stadium began in the same district, less than a kilometre away from
the old one.

It opened in 1957 and soon came
to be known as the Camp Nou (New
Stadium) because nobody could
agree on an official name. With a
93,000-spectator capacity, it became
Europe's largest all-seater stadium, a
position that was reinforced following

an extension in 1981 which saw
its capacity increase to 120,000. It
didn't lose this status, despite a subsequent reduction to the current capacity
of 99,000 carried out to comply with
safety standards stipulating that all
spectators must have a seat.

Originally designed by the architect Francesc Mitjans, Camp Nou
has hosted matches from the 1964
European Nations Cup, the 1982 World
Cup (the third grandstand was built for
the event), the 1992 Olympic Games
and the 1989 and 1999 European Cup
finals, as well as huge concerts by such
famous names as Michael Jackson,
Bruce Springsteen and U2.

However, Camp Nou is best known
as the home ground of FC Barcelona,
one of the world's most prestigious
clubs which has won European titles
in football, basketball, handball and
ice hockey. That's why the stadium and
its adjoining museum – which takes a
thorough look at the history of the club
and showcases all its trophies – have
become Barcelona's second most visited tourist attraction, only surpassed
by the Sagrada Família.

Barcelona

Practical guide

Getting there

Barcelona has excellent transport links with the rest of Spain and Europe and operates intercontinental flights with America and Asia.

By plane

Most flights arrive at Barcelona Airport (**Aeroport del Prat-Barcelona**, T 93 298 38 38; www.aena.es), 12 km from the city centre. Connections: journey time 35 min, **Aerobús A1** to **terminal T1** every 5 min, from 5.30 am to 1.05am, and **Aerobús A2** to **terminals T2B** and **T2C** every 10 min from 5.30am to 1am (www.aerobusbcn.com); journey time 26 min, train on **R2** line to **terminal T2** (free shuttle bus – journey time 10 min – to terminal T1) every 30 min, from 5.21am to 11.38pm (T 902 240 202); and taxi (journey time 30 min). Some low-cost airlines use **Girona Airport** (T 972 186 600; www.aena.es), 80 km away. Connections: buses timed to tie in with flight arrivals and departures (T 902 361 550; www.sagales.com / journey time 70 min); and **Reus Airport** (T 977 779 800; www.aena.es), 80 km away. Connections: Bus Hispano Igualadina (T 938 044 451).

By train

Rail links with most cities in the rest of Spain and Europe depart from and arrive at **Barcelona-Sants Station**. The rail operator is the state-owned company RENFE (T 902 240 202; www.renfe.es) and many connections are by high-speed train.

By bus

The main intercity bus station is the **Estació del Nord** (T 902 260 606; www.barcelonanord.com), although many international services depart from Sants Station. The companies include Eurolines (T 902 40 50 40; www.eurolines.es), Alsa Internacional (T 902 422 242; www.alsa.es) and Linebús (T 93 265 07 00).

By boat

Barcelona operates regular ferry services with the Balearic Islands: Acciona-Trasmediterránea (T 902 454 645; www.trasmediterranea.es), Balearia (www.balearia.com), Iscomar (www.iscomar.com); Italy: Grimaldi-lines, Grandi Navi Veloci, Condemar; and Algeria, Tangiers and Oran (Condemar and Canam). The city has also become Europe's leading cruise port, with annual passenger figures of one and a half million.

Language

Barcelona is a bilingual city where Catalan and Spanish are spoken.

Catalan

Catalan is the language of Barcelona, the rest of Catalonia, the Balearic Islands, Valencia (where it is called *valencià*) and

More than 100 domestic and international airlines operate almost 900 daily flights to more than 150 destinations throughout the world. Barcelona Airport's T1 terminal opened in June 2009 and can handle 55 million passengers a year and 90 flights an hour, making it the leading airport in the Aena network in terms of traffic. Its facilities include one of the most advanced retail spaces in Europe which offers an innovative range of exclusive services, a wide range of shops selling prestigious brands and a wide variety of bars and restaurants, one of them run by a Michelin-starred chef.

Andorra. It is spoken by eight million people. Its use is widespread in such areas of public life as street and road signs, signage systems, maps, restaurant menus, etc.

Spanish
Spanish, or Castilian, is also an official language and is spoken by all Catalan speakers.

Other languages
Quite a few people in Barcelona understand English and French. A lot of restaurants have menus in other languages and public transport signs are also in English.

Banks and money
As in 15 other European Union countries, the official currency is the euro (€).

Banks and saving banks
Banking hours are 8.30am-2pm, Monday to Friday. From September to June, banks also open on Saturday from 8am to 2pm, and savings banks (*caixes* in Catalan and *cajas* in Spanish) open on Thursday afternoons from 4pm to 8pm. There are banks at the airport and at Barcelona-Sants Station, which open daily

from 8am to 10pm. The city also has one of the most extensive networks of ATM machines in the world, and Visa, MasterCard and American Express can be used to make cash withdrawals.

Changing money
Currency can be exchanged at banks, savings banks and bureaux de change. Commission rates vary.

Credit cards and travellers' cheques
Visa and MasterCard are accepted everywhere, with the exception of some small shops and restaurants; most hotels take American Express; and 50% of restaurants take Diner's Card. Travellers' cheques can be changed at all banks or bureaux de change.

Food and drink
Mealtimes in Barcelona (and the rest of Catalonia and Spain) are a little later than the rest of Europe. Lunchtime is between 2pm and 3pm and dinner from 9pm onwards.

Restaurants
Most restaurants open from 1pm to 4pm and from 8pm to 11pm, but many remain open all day, and

some serve dinner until 2am. They usually close on one day a week and some close in August.

Cafés and bars
They usually open at about 7.30am and close at 2am. You can also have a drink at nightclubs and discotheques after this time. Some of them also serve food.

Shopping
Over the past decade, Barcelona has become a European haven for shoppers (see p. 84). Most shops open from 10am to 2pm and 4pm to 9pm, Monday to Friday, although few shops in the city centre close for lunch. Department stores and shopping centres open from 10am to 10pm, Monday to Saturday. Some shops open 365 days a year from 8am to 2am. Here you can find a wide variety of products: food, drinks, CDs, books, gifts, clothes, cleaning and beauty products, flowers, etc. The most centrally located ones are at Ronda Sant Pere, 33; Ronda Sant Pau, 34 and Gran de Gràcia, 29.

Sales
There are two sales

Cruise liner in the harbour

Having lunch on the Passeig Marítim

Practical guide

periods: in summer, from 1st July to the end of August, and in winter, from 7th January to the end of February.

Fira del Bellcaire
Barcelona also has a flea market with a long-standing tradition, known locally as Els Encants Vells. Its origins can be traced back to the 14th century, and it has stood on its current site in the Plaça de les Glòries since 1928. It covers a surface area of more than 15,000 m². www.encantsbcn.com

Public holidays
Shops and banks are closed on Sundays, 1st and 6th January, Good Friday, Easter Monday, 1st May, 24th June, 15th August, 11th and 24th September, 12th October, 1st November and 6th, 8th, 25th and 26th December. (www.gencat.cat/especial/comerc/eng/index.htm)

Climate

Barcelona enjoys a privileged Mediterranean climate with mild winters and warm, occasionally wet summers. The average winter temperature is 12°C (54°F) and it seldom rains. Summer temperatures usually reach 30°C (86°F), and are often higher. There are occasional storms. Spring and autumn (average temperatures of 21°C, 70°F) are the best times to visit the city, although it does rain more often.

Festivals

In addition to Christmas, New Year and Epiphany, Barcelona celebrates other festivals which are bursting with typical Mediterranean vitality. Winter is Carnival time, with a big parade in the city. In spring, Sant Jordi (Saint George's Day) is a unique celebration focusing on a passion for books and roses. In summer, Sant Joan (Saint John) has bonfires and fireworks as its centrepiece. The 11th September is the Diada (Catalan National Day) and after this, it's time for La Mercè, Barcelona's main festival, packed with cultural events, traditional folklore and festivities.

Many neighbourhoods in the city (Gràcia, Sants, Ciutat Vella...) hold their own festivals (www.bcn.cat/festes).

Local culture
Be sure not to miss traditional folklore displays including the Catalan folk dance, the *sardana* (www.fed.sardanista.cat), human castles, *castells* (www.castellersdebarcelona.cat) and *diables* (processions of masked devils who run through the crowd letting off fireworks; www.diables.cat).

Beaches

Barcelona has more than 4.5 km of Blue Flag beaches (which comply with EU standards regarding water quality, environmental management and education, safety and services), that can be used all year round because of the mild climate, although the official bathing season (when all services are provided, including disabled access, the loan of newspapers, books, sporting equipment and

Encants Vells

Castells

children's toys) is from 15th There is a bathing area for nudists.
www.bcn.cat/platges

Mountains

Collserola Natural Park (and its hill Tibidabo) are not as well-known as the city's beaches but they are a popular place with locals when they want to get away from the bustle of the city.

Here you can walk close to nature along the Carretera de les Aigües, which commands the finest views of the city, have a bite to eat at one of the open-air snack bars in Les Planes (just 20 min from Pl. Catalunya on lines S1, S2 and S5 of Catalan railways, FGC: www.fgc. cat) or go on a number of hiking routes, bicycle and horse rides (www. parccollserola.net).

Gay friendly

Barcelona is an open, tolerant city and is in the top ten of the world's gay-friendly cities. The most important area is the Gayxample, a rectangle bounded by the streets of Gran Via, Aragó, Aribau and Villarroel. (www. gaybarcelona.net). Turisme de Barcelona publishes a guide.

Safety and healthcare

As in every major city, there are places (public transport, etc.) where you should keep an eye on your belongings. The emergency telephone number is 112, as in the rest of the European Union. In Barcelona, calls are dealt with in Catalan, Spanish, English and French and there is a translation service in other languages. The number is used to contact the police, fire brigade and ambulance service.

Police

Other emergency numbers include 088, the Catalan Police (Mossos d'Esquadra); 091, Spanish Police (Policía Nacional); and 092, local police (Guàrdia Urbana). There is a help centre for tourists at 43, La Rambla which opens 24 hours a day (T 93 256 24 30) to help visitors who have been victims of crime or have had an accident.

Hospitals

There are many hospitals in Barcelona, some of them renowned throughout the world. These are some of the most important. They all have an A & E department: Hospital de Sant Pau (Sant Antoni M. Claret, 167. T 93 291 90 00), Hospital Clínic (Villarroel, 170. T 93 227 54 00), Hospital Dos de Maig (Dos de Maig, 301. T 93 507 27 00), Hospital de la Vall d'Hebron (Passeig de la Vall d'Hebron, 119-129. T 93 489 30 00) and Hospital del Mar (Passeig Marítim, 25-29. T 93 248 30 00).

Ambulances

The 061 number deals with all ambulance calls.

Chemists

These are the only places in BCN where you can buy medicinal drugs dispensed by qualified pharmacists. They also stock homoeopathic medicines and have an illuminated green cross outside. They open from 9am to 2pm and from 4pm and 8pm. All neighbourhoods have duty chemists that are open all night (the rota is displayed on the door of every chemists). There are increasing numbers of 24-hour chemists, particularly in the city centre.

Carretera de les Aigües

Vila Olímpica beach

Practical guide

History

Before the Romans

Although the oldest surviving remains of human settlements on the Barcelona plain date from Neolithic times (5000 BC), the city has its origins in the Laietan tribe of the Iberians (6th century BC), who founded a settlement called Barkeno.

Barcino

The *Colonia Iulia Augusta Paterna Faventia Barcino* was founded circa 10 BC under the protection of Emperor Augustus. The colony is described in documents dating from the 2nd century (Pliny and Ptolemy) as a pleasant place, with fertile land and a small harbour. The city has a classic colonial walled layout, with four gateways which marked the entrance to the *decumanus* (now Carrer del Bisbe and Carrer de la Ciutat) and the *cardo* (Carrer del Call and Carrer de la Llibreteria), which converged in the centre, or forum (Plaça de St. Jaume).

Early Roman era

Between the 2nd and 4th centuries, the city enjoyed a major period of prosperity and its products (wine and *garum* – a fish-based sauce) were sold throughout the empire. The second wall (the one we can see today) dates from the end of this period and saw the arrival of an important Christian community, whose bishops were the true defenders of the Roman civilisation.

Visigothic rule

In 415, the Visigothic king Ataülf established his court in the city, and, with the fall of the Roman Empire (476), Barcino came under the rule of the Visigothic kingdom of Toulouse and was then governed by the Peninsular kingdoms.

From Islamic to Carolingian rule

In 717, the city came under Islamic rule, although it retained its civic and religious authorities. It became part of Emperor Charlemagne's empire in 797 and his son Louis the Pious conquered the city in 801, establishing the county of Barcelona as part of the Hispanic Marches.

The city of the counts

The counts of Barcelona gradually distanced themselves from Frankish rule. In 985, the city was attacked by a Muslim army led by Al-Mansur, and when the Frankish king declined to intervene, Count Borrell II refused to recognise the king's sovereignty, an action that marked the beginning of independence for the region that would later be called Catalonia. In 1137, Ramon Berenguer IV married Petronella of Aragon and their son, Alfons II, became the first king of Aragon and count of Barcelona. Both

Museu d'Arqueologia de Catalunya

El Call

Barcino. Joan Brossa

territories kept their courts, languages and laws.

The medieval golden age
Jaume I, the Conqueror (1208-1276) took Mallorca, Menorca, Valencia and Murcia from the Muslims, marking the start of a phase during which Barcelona became the hub of maritime trade in Europe in the Middle Ages. The Gothic Quarter bears witness to this period.

Consell de Cent
Jaume I founded a municipal government in Barcelona, which first sat in 1265: three councillors elected by a council of 100 eminent people (noblemen, merchants, artists and craftsmen). It is considered to be the first European parliament.

Generalitat
The origins of the Catalan government, the Generalitat de Catalunya, can be traced back to the Catalan Parliament, or Corts, which was made up of representatives of different social groups.

1714
The War of the Spanish Succession divided Europe between the supporters of the Bourbon, Philippe of Anjou (France and Castile) and those of Archduke Charles of Austria (England, Austria, the Netherlands and the territories of the Crown of Aragon). The Bourbon victory led to the abolition of self-government in Catalonia and Barcelona.

Renaixença
In the mid-19th century, following a long period of decline, the industrial revolution triggered great economic prosperity (culminating in the 1888 Universal Exhibition) and Barcelona spearheaded a powerful cultural movement which revived the Catalan language and the notion of a Catalan nation. This had major political repercussions resulting in movements that reinforced the Catalan identity.

Modernisme
Catalonia's home-grown art nouveau, *modernisme*, was adopted as something of a national style in Barcelona and Catalonia after the *Renaixença*. The movement produced architectural landmarks of great artistic value.

20th century
Barcelona experienced many changes in fortune throughout this century.

The Republic
The first 30 years of the century were a period of turmoil and political revolution cut short by the start of the Civil War in 1936.

Dictatorship
After the victory of the fascists (1939), Barcelona, which had remained loyal to the Republic until the bitter end, endured great hardship. However, slow economic and cultural recovery began towards the end of the 1950s, as a result of which the city led the fight for democracy in the 1970s.

Democracy
With the reinstatement of civil liberties and autonomy, the city embarked on a period of urban renewal and social cohesion which has created a model that is universal in scope.

Olympic Barcelona
The 1992 Olympics were a milestone in the aforementioned process of renewal which has continued into the 21st century with the hosting of the Forum of Cultures and the city's confirmation as the headquarters of the Union for the Mediterranean.
www.bcn.cat

Museu d'Història de Barcelona

Practical guide

Visit BCN with discounts

Barcelona Card

The best option for 2, 3, 4 or 5 days. Includes a guide in Catalan/Spanish/English and French/Italian/German. Free travel on public transport: TMB metro and city buses, FGC city lines, trams, airport train, zone 1 Renfe suburban rail. Almost 100 discounts and free offers at museums, cultural and leisure attractions, nights-clubs, shops, restaurants and on entertainment, unique means of transport and other services. For sales and detailed information www.barcelonaturisme.cat

Transport

Barcelona has an extensive underground railway (metro and FGC) and bus network which serves the whole city. www.tmb.net and www.fgc.cat

Travel cards

They allow you to travel throughout the entire public transport network and can be purchased at metro stations, tourist offices and on-line. T-2 Dies (2-day pass - 11.20 €), T-3 Dies (3-day pass - 15.90 €), T-4 Dies (4-day pass 20.40 €) and T-5 Dies (5-day pass - 24.10 €), which offer unlimited travel on the days indicated.

Barcelona Bus Turístic

The most convenient way of discovering the city's most attractive sights and landmarks on three routes. Price: 23 €, 1 day (children, 14 €) and 30 €, 2 days (children, 18 €). The same ticket can be used on all three routes. Includes an informative guide describing each stop and a discount-voucher booklet to be used at the main landmarks and attractions. There is also the night-time Barcelona Bus Turístic, which runs in summer and reveals the beauty of Barcelona's landmark buildings floodlit at night, and the Magic Fountain on Montjuïc. Friday, Saturday and Sunday, May to September.

Metro Walks

Seven routes combining travel on the metro, city walks and bus or tram rides, to discover Barcelona from an insider's point of view, as well as its history, neighbourhoods, urban development... as if you were one of the locals, at your own pace. Includes a guide featuring the routes, maps and public transport. www.barcelonaturisme.cat

Museums

ArtTicket

Single ticket providing admission to seven BCN museums and art centres: Centre de Cultura Contemporània de Barcelona (CCCB); Fundació Antoni Tàpies; Fundació Caixa Catalunya-La Pedrera; Fundació Joan Miró; Museu Nacional d'Art de Catalunya (MNAC); Museu d'Art Contemporani de Barcelona-MACBA and Museu Picasso. Valid for six months from purchase date. Price: 25 €.

ArqueoTicket

Multi-ticket providing admission to BCN's five archaeological museums: Museu d'Arqueologia de Catalunya; Museu Barbier-Mueller d'Art Precolombí de Barcelona; Museu Egipci de Barcelona; Museu d'Història de Barcelona and Museu Marítim de Barcelona. Valid for one year from purchase date. Price: 14 €.

Ticket Ciència

Single ticket providing admission to seven science museums: Museu de Ciències Naturals, CosmoCaixa, Museu Agbar, Botanical Gardens, Museu Marítim, Museu de la Ciència i la Tècnica de Catalunya and the zoo. Valid for one year from purchase date. Price: 18.50 €. The three tickets are on sale at the city's museums, tourist offices and on-line at www.barcelonaturisme.cat

Others

Montjuïc Card

Experience Montjuïc (museums, swimming pools, cable car, bicycles...) for one day. Price: 20 € (children, 10 €). www.bcn.cat/sants-montjuic.

Youth and student discount cards

Holders of the International Student Card (ISIC: www.isic.org) and the Euro26 card (www.euro26.org) can obtain discounts at the main landmarks and attractions.

Senior citizens

People aged over 65 are entitled to discounts on a wide range of services.

Other offers

www.barcelonaturisme.cat

Trade fairs and congresses

Barcelona's geographical location, economic and cultural vibrancy and the quality of its services and infrastructures have made it the leading international congress city in the south of Europe. The Barcelona International Convention Centre is one of the main venues and won the M&IT Silver Award for the best congress facility of 2008. www.ccib.es (auditorium: 3,155 seats).
Other venues include the Catalonia Congress Centre (auditorium: 2,000 seats) www.pcongresos.com and the Barcelona Congress Centre (auditorium: 1,650 seats). www. firabcn.es. Fira de Barcelona is the biggest trade-fair site in Spain and one of Europe's leading exhibition facilities. It hosts 80 trade shows with 40,000 businesses participating, and attracting four million visitors. It hosts 15 of Europe's benchmark trade fairs. These include **Construmat** (the third most important in Europe); **Alimentaria** (ranks second in the world); **Mobile World Congress** (the biggest mobile technology fair); **EIBTM** (the global meetings and incentive exhibition); and **The Brandery, Post Fashion Circus** and **080 Barcelona Fashion** (creative streetwear). www.firabcn.es

Festivals

Throughout the year, Barcelona hosts hundreds of festivals devoted to the arts, music, theatre, dance, film, audiovisuals...
Grec. BCN Festival
June to August. A showcase for classic and groundbreaking plays, dance, music and circus performances. www.barcelonafestival.com

Sónar
The world's leading Festival of Advanced Music and Multimedia Art. www.sonar.es
Primavera Sound
The best and most innovative music from the indie, folk, pop and rock scene. www.primaverasound.com

BAM
Held during Barcelona's main festival. Free concerts by groups from Spain and abroad at different venues around the city. www.bcn.cat/bam

Other music festivals
Festival Internacional de Jazz
www.theproject.es
Festival de Flamenco
www.flamencociutatvella.com
Festival Internacional de Percusión
www.auditori.org
Festival de Guitarra de Barcelona
www.theproject.es
Festival de Música Antiga
www.auditori.org
Hipnotik
www.hipnotikfestival.com
Weekend Dance
www.weekendance.es
Mas i Mas Festival
www.masimas.com/festival

Sónar Festival

Barcelona Shopping Line

If you love shopping, you'll love Barcelona. The city is home to the famous **Barcelona Shopping Line**, the 5-km retail thoroughfare with 35,000 shops where you'll find every item imaginable. It begins at Ciutat Vella, goes through the Plaça de Catalunya, up the Passeig de Gràcia and along the Diagonal. Most of the area is pedestrianised so it's a pleasant experience to go from shop to shop without worrying about the traffic and to enjoy some of the city's most attractive and iconic landmarks. The Barcelona Shopping Line features a wide variety of shops, which includes leading brands such as Versace, Armani, Burberry, Bally, Cartier, Calvin Klein, Armand Basi, Antonio Miró, Custo, Mango, Furest and Adolfo Domínguez, to name just some (www.barcelonaturisme.cat/bsl)

Shopping centres and department stores

The most characterful shops are highlighted in each area in the guide. Below you'll find a list of the major shopping centres which have cafés and restaurants, entertainment complexes, shops selling clothes, accessories, shoes, decorative goods, jewellery, sporting goods, toys, perfumes, computers, phones, souvenirs, etc.

1. El Corte Inglés
Pl. de Catalunya, 14
Av. Portal de l'Àngel, 19
Av. Diagonal, 617
Av. Diagonal, 471-473
Pg. d'Andreu Nin, 51
www.elcorteingles.es
Since 1935. Spain's department store par excellence.

2. Pedralbes Centre
Av. Diagonal, 609-615
www.pedralbescentre.com

3. L'Illa Diagonal
Av. Diagonal, 545- 565
www.lilla.com

4. Bulevard Rosa
Passeig de Gràcia, 53
www.bulevardrosa.com

5. El Triangle
Plaça Catalunya, 1-4
www.eltriangle.es

6. Maremagnum
Moll de Espanya, 5
www.maremagnum.es

7. Poble Espanyol
Av. Marquès de Comillas, s/n
www.poble-espanyol.com

8. Barcelona Glòries
Av. Diagonal, 208
www.lesglories.com

9. Les Arenes
Plaça d'Espanya

www.arenasdebarcelona. com

10. Diagonal Mar
www.diagonalmarcentre.es

11. Heron City
Av. Río de Janeiro, 42
www.heroncitybarcelona. com

12. La Maquinista
Passeig de Potosí, 2
www.lamaquinista.com

13. La Roca Village
Exit 12 (Cardedeu) of the AP7 motorway
www.larocavillage.com
Prestigious fashion labels from Spain and abroad with up to 60% off the R.R.P. Set out in an attractive shopping village.

Retail areas

The shopkeepers' associations in the different neighbourhoods of BCN have created a series of dynamic retail areas which pay special attention to customer service. There are 16 of these areas at the present time, including Sants-Creu Coberta (which is considered the world's longest shopping street), Sant Andreu, Gran de Gràcia and the Cor d'Horta. www.eixosbcn.net

Tax-free

Travellers residing outside the EU are entitled to a refund of the VAT paid on purchases in the city, provided that the cost of the goods exceeds 90.15 € (hotels and restaurants are excluded). Ask the shop assistant for a tax-free cheque and on leaving the EU present the goods along with the cheque at customs. You can cash your cheque in a number of ways, according to the options provided by the participating outlet at the airport or EU borders. You can also obtain a cash refund before you leave at the Turisme de Barcelona Information Office in Plaça Catalunya. For further information, visit www. barcelonaturisme.cat/bsl and www.global-blue.com

Shop window display

Practical guide

Gastronomy

Gastronomy is one of the mainstays of Catalan culture. The region's famous chefs have made Barcelona synonymous with an extraordinary culinary treasure trove, which is varied and of high quality. Here is a selection of the city's restaurants (+60 €) which will give you the chance to sample peerless cuisine. (*), (**) or (***) indicates Michelin-starred restaurants in 2010.

ÀBAC *
Avinguda Tibidabo, 1
T 93 319 66 00
Dining rooms in every shade of white provide the backdrop to the creative cuisine of Jordi Cruz.

ALKÍMIA *
Indústria, 79
T 93 207 61 15
Jordi Vilà is one of the new Catalan chefs who are amazing the world with their recreations of traditional Catalan cuisine.

CAELIS **
Gran Via, 668
T 93 510 12 05
At the Hotel El Palace, the chef Romain Fornell serves his innovative and delicious Mediterranean cuisine in a luxury restaurant.

CINC SENTITS *
Aribau, 58
T 93 323 94 90
A unique take on contemporary Catalan cuisine with creative touches from around the world.

CASA LEOPOLDO
Sant Rafael, 24
T 93 441 30 14
Legendary restaurant in the Raval. Since 1929. Frequented by artists and intellectuals. It has a 50 € tasting menu.

COMERÇ 24 *
Comerç, 24
T 93 319 21 02
Carles Abellan, who worked with Ferran Adrià, has raised traditional tapas and tasting dishes to the highest levels of modern cuisine.

DOS CIELOS *
Pere IV, 272-286
T 93 367 20 70
From the 24th floor of the Hotel Me with impressive views, signature haute cuisine by the brothers Javier and Sergio Torres.

DROLMA *
Passeig de Gràcia, 68
T 93 496 77 10
Sophistication and luxury at the Hotel Majestic. The chef, Fermí Puig, creates a world of flavours and culinary sensations.

ENOTECA *
Marina, 19-21
T 93 221 10 00
Signature cuisine by the chef Paco Pérez. "The freshness of the sea and the essence of the produce".

EL PASSADÍS D'EN PEP
Pla de Palau, 2
T 93 310 10 21
Seafood cuisine at one of the city's finest shellfish restaurants. It is supplied by six fishing harbours.

EVO *
Gran Via Corts Catalanes, 154
T 93 413 50 30
The famous chef Santi Santamaria (El Racó de Can Fabes). 100 metres above the city.

FONDA GAIG
Còrsega, 200
T 93 453 20 20
Carles Gaig goes back to the clean and intense flavours of traditional Catalan dishes at his new restaurant.

FREIXA TRADICIÓ
Sant Elies, 22
T 93 209 75 59
Ramon Freixa injects his dishes with an amazing creative skill. The enfant terrible of Barcelona's chefs.

GAIG *
Aragó, 214
T 93 429 10 17
Originally housed in an inn founded in Horta in 1869. Carles Gaig has brought his traditional dishes to the centre of Barcelona.

GALAXÓ
Passeig de Gràcia, 132
T 93 255 30 00
Housed in the modernista hotel Casa Fuster, it offers an innovative Mediterranean menu of signature dishes.

HISOP *
Passatge Marimón, 9
T 93 241 32 33
Two young chefs dazzle us with their contemporary Catalan cuisine.

HOFFMAN *
La Granada del Penedès, 14
T 93 218 71 65
Mey Hofmann creates and recreates dishes which retain all the essence, flavour and aroma of the raw ingredients.

LASARTE **
Mallorca, 259
T 93 445 32 42
Open since 2006, it has already received two Michelin stars. Its chef, Martín Berasategui, has a 3-Michelin-starred restaurant in Guipúzcoa (Basque Country).

LLUÇANÈS *
Plaça de la Font, s/n
T 93 224 25 25
Creative signature cuisine from the chef Àngel Pasqual. Housed in the Barceloneta Market since 2007.

MANAIRÓ *
Diputació, 424
T 93 231 00 57
Creative Catalan cuisine

with a highly personal touch.

MOMENTS *
Passeig de Gràcia, 38
T 93 151 88 88
Traditional yet modern Catalan cuisine by Carme Ruscalleda (5 Michelin stars) and her son Raül Balam.

MONVÍNIC
Diputació, 249
T 93 272 61 87
Perhaps the best wine bar in the world with a dining area run by the chef Sergi de Meià.

MOO *
Rosselló, 265
T 93 445 40 00
The Roca brothers, who have a 2-starred Michelin restaurant in Girona, develop their vision of Catalan haute cuisine.

NEICHEL *
Beltrán i Rózpide, 1-5
T 93 203 84 08
After working alongside renowned French and German chefs, Jean Louis Neichel obtained his first star in 1976.

ROIG ROBÍ
Sèneca, 20
T 93 218 92 22
With a delightful terrace and garden. Mercè Navarro and her daughter Imma prepare family recipes with modern criteria.

SAÜC *
Via Laietana, 49
T 93 321 01 89
Housed in the new Ohla Hotel, its young chef, Xavi Franco, hasn't lost sight of his Catalan culinary roots.

TORRE D'ALTA MAR
Passeig Joan de Borbó, 88
T 93 221 00 07
75m above sea level, this restaurant with its cutting-edge design offers traditional Mediterranean delicacies.

VIA VENETO *
Ganduxer, 10
T 93 200 72 44
Impeccable service. Since 1967, its classic Catalan cuisine has been renowned for its innovative touches and dependability.

Less than 45 minutes away:

EL RACÓ DE CAN FABES ***
Sant Joan, 6 (Sant Celoni)
T 93 867 28 51

SANT PAU ***
Nou, 10 (Sant Pol de Mar)
T 93 760 06 62

CAN JUBANY *
Ctra. de Sant Hilari, s/n (Calldetenes)
T 93 889 10 23

EL CINGLE *
Pl. Major, s/n (Vacarisses)
T 93 828 02 33

L'ANGLE *
Món Sant Benet
(St. Fruitós de Bages)
T 672 208 691

SALA *
Plaça Major, 17 (Olost)
T 93 888 01 06

Market Trail

Barcelona's food markets are dynamic spaces. There's no better way to meet the locals than walking round the city's markets, chatting to the stallholders and buying some produce. The city has a network of more than 40 markets, among which we highlight the Boqueria, named the world's Market of the Year in Washington in 2006. The website www.bcn. cat/mercatsmunicipals features four walking trails, which include *Modernista* Markets, visiting five markets built between 1888 and 1913, most of them made of brick and wrought iron and classified as listed buildings; and **Landmark Markets**, which includes the Boqueria, Santa Caterina and Barceloneta, the latter two having recently undergone spectacular refurbishments.

89 **Colour, flavour, aroma**

Modernista shield

Nightlife and entertainment

Theatre

Barcelona is a city with a long-standing theatrical tradition, particularly where independent and avant-garde performances are concerned. Some of its companies (**La Fura dels Baus**, **Comedians** and **Tricicle**) are known throughout the world. Others, such as the **Teatre Lliure**, **La Cubana** and **Dagoll Dagom**, have earned great prestige in Europe. The city has 27 theatres (ranging from 3,000-seater venues for musicals to smaller pocket-theatre venues seating under 100), which include two major publicly funded complexes: the **Teatre Nacional de Catalunya** (Pl. de les Arts, 1; T 93 306 57 00; www.tnc.cat) opened in 1996, It has three theatre spaces seating 870, 450 and 400 people respectively; and the **Ciutat del Teatre** (located in 19th-century-style buildings constructed for the 1929 International Exhibition), which includes the **Mercat de les Flors-Centre de les Arts de Moviment** (Lleida, 59; T 93 426 18 75; www.mercatflors.org) which opened in 1985 as a theatre and is now a dance venue. It has two theatre spaces seating 664 and 80 people; and the **Teatre Lliure** (Pl. de Santa Madrona, 40-46; T 93 228 97 47; www.teatrelliure.com) which opened in 2001 and has two venues seating 736 and 172 people.

Musicals

A few years ago, the city revived the genre and now hosts musicals by international companies as well as home-grown productions which can be seen at Barcelona Teatre Musical, the Tivoli, the Victòria and other venues.

El Paral·lel
The avenue with a theatrical flavour. See p. 29

Film

Barcelona has 29 cinemas with more than 170 screens showing 80 films every day. Original-language-version films are screened at **Renoir Floridablanca** (Floridablanca, 135); **Renoir Les Corts** (Eugeni d'Ors, 12); **Verdi** (Verdi, 32); **Verdi Park** (Torrijos, 49) and **Yelmo Icària** (Salvador Espriu, 61).

Music
Classical

Barcelona has three major

Teatre Nacional de Catalunya

Gran Teatre del Liceu

World music concert

venues. Two of them are historic landmarks known by music-lovers from around the world. They are the **Gran Teatre del Liceu**, (Rambla, 51-59; T 93 485 99 00; www.liceubarcelona.com), which has been one of the main opera houses since the 19th century, and the **Palau de la Música Catalana** (Palau de la Música, 4-6; T 902 442 882; www.palaumusica.cat), a *modernista* masterpiece which is considered the world's most beautiful concert hall. The third, **L'Auditori** (Lepant, 150; T 93 247 93 00; www.auditori.org) is a modern building designed by the architect Rafael Moneo and the home of the Orquestra Simfònica de Barcelona i Nacional de Catalunya.

Jazz

The city has a thriving jazz community (local talents and musicians from other cities such as NY and London) (www.urbaanjazz.com). Make sure you visit **Jamboree** (Pl. Reial, 17; www.masimas.com/jamboree); **The Jazz Room** (Vallmajor, 33; www.masimas.com/jazzroom); **DosTrece** (Carme, 40; www.dostrece.net); **Harlem Jazz Club** (Comtessa de Sobradiel, 8); **Jazz Sí** (Requesens, 2); **Bel·luna Jazz-Club** (Rambla Catalunya, 5; www.bel-luna.com)

Flamenco

Barcelona has one of the most dynamic flamenco scenes in the country and is always receptive to up-and-coming artists whether they perform classic or new-style flamenco. **Tablao Cordobés** (La Rambla, 35; www.tablaocordobes.com); **Tarantos** (Pl. Reial, 17; www.masimas.com); **El Tablao de Carmen** (Av. Marquès de Comillas, s/n; www.tablaodecarmen.com).

Clubs

Barcelona is a cosmopolitan city with a groundbreaking, vibrant club scene. Many of its venues are known throughout Europe. They host live concerts and DJ sets. Some have restaurants and several dance floors playing different styles of music until 4am. **Razzmatazz/The Loft** (Pamplona, 88; www.salarazzmatazz.com); **Otto Zutz** (Lincoln, 15; www.ottozutz.es); **Red Lounge** (Pg. Joan de Borbó, 78; www.redloungebcn.com); **Space** (Tarragona, 141-147; www.spacebarcelona.com); **Sala Apolo** (Nou de la Rambla, 111-113; www.sala-apolo.com); **Pacha** (Dr. Marañón, 17; www.clubpachabcn.com); **Moog** (Arc del Teatre, 3; www.masimas.com); **Shôko Lounge Club** (P. Marítim, 36, www.shoko.biz); **Duvet** (Còrsega, 327; www.duvet.es); **Broadbar** (Aribau, 191; www.broadbar.com); **Luz de Gas** (Muntaner, 246; www.luzdegas.com); **Arena Classic** (Diputació, 233; gay friendly; www.arenadisco.com); **Arena Vip** (Gran Via, 593); **Bikini** (Av. Diagonal, 547; www.bikinibcn.com); **Zac Club** (Diagonal, 477; www.zac-club.com); **Elephant** (Passeig dels Til·lers, 1; www.elephantbcn.com); **Sidecar** (Pl. Reial, 7; www.sidecarfactory.com); **Belly** (Casanova, 48; gay friendly); **Dietrich** (Consell de Cent, 255; gay friendly); **Metro** (Sepúlveda, 185; www.metrodiscobcn.com; gay friendly); **Magic Club** (Passeig Picasso, 40; www.magic-club.net).

Palau de la Música Catalana

Flamenco

Razzmatazz

Practical guide

Sport

Barcelona's passion for sport dates back to the late 19th century, when it introduced a wide range of sporting specialities to Spain. This tradition has endowed the city with many sports clubs, some of them founded over 100 years ago, culminating in the Olympic Games. Turisme de Barcelona's **Barcelona Sports** programme publishes a guide featuring the main international sporting events. Barcelona is in great shape. Experience our city through sport!

Football
Champions League
FC Barcelona will be taking part in top-level European competitions, as it does nearly every year. For matches, visit www.uefa.com
First Division
Two century-old clubs, FC Barcelona and RCD Espanyol, play on alternate weekends in one of the world's top football leagues. To buy tickets, hire a box or VIP seat: www.fcbarcelona.cat and www.rcdespanyol.com.
Tournaments
The city hosts the 44th **Joan Gamper Estrella Damm Trophy** (www.fcbarcelona.cat) and the 36th **Ciutat de Barcelona Trophy** (www.rcdespanyol.com) during the second fortnight in August.

Motor sports
The **Spanish Formula 1 Grand Prix** is held in May (www.circuitcat.com) from 8th to 10th May.
June: the **Cinzano Catalan Grand Prix**, which is part

of the **World Motorcycle Championship** for 125 cc, Moto 2 and MotoGP classes (www.circuitcat.com).
January: the 32nd **Barcelona Indoor Trial**, the first in this speciality. www.rpmracing.com
Practice
Circuit de Catalunya
www.circuitcat.com
T 93 571 97 00
The public can hire cars and motorcycles for 30-minute practice sessions all year round. See website for times and prices.

Tennis
At the end of April, the Real Club de Tenis Barcelona will be hosting the **Barcelona Open Sabadell Atlántico - 57th Conde de Godó Trophy** (www.rctb1899.es), Spain's oldest tennis tournament. ATP World Tour 500. The club was founded in 1899.
Practice
Club de Tennis Vall Parc (www.vallparc.com; T 93 212 67 89); **Nova Icària Esports** (Av. Icària, 167 T 93 221 25 80); **Tennis Pompeia** (Foixarda s/n, Montjuïc; T 93 325 13 48); **Club Bonasport** (Vista Bella, 11; T 93 254 15 00).

Equestrian sports
In February, the city will be hosting the 98th **International Showjumping Competition** (www.csiobarcelona.com), which is part of the Samsung SuperLeague (the top eight competitions on the world showjumping calendar). It is organised by the Real Club de Polo de Barcelona, founded in

1897. www.rcpb.com
Practice
Escola Municipal d'Hípica (Av. Muntanyans, 1; T 93 426 10 66); **Hípica Sant Cugat** (www.hipicasantcugat.es; T 616 868 881); **Hípica Sant Pau d'Ordal** (www.hipicasantpau.com; T 938 993 029).

Golf
Practice
On Montjuïc, includes equipment hire. On Sunday, Green Fee Pitch&Putt. Times and prices: www.golfmontjuic.com

Yachting
In May, the city will be hosting the 36th **Conde de Godó Regatta Trophy** (www.regatagodo.com); organised by the Real Club Náutico de Barcelona, which was founded over 130 years ago (www.rcnb.com). The city will be hosting the 2nd **Barcelona World Race** on 31st December 2010. An unassisted, non-stop race covering more than 25,000 miles (www.barcelonaworldrace.org).
Practice
Centre Municipal de Vela (Moll de Gregal, s/n; T 93 225 79 40); **Base Nàutica** (Av. Litoral, s/n; T 93 221 04 32).

Cycling
In May the city will be hosting the Volta Ciclista a Catalunya (www.voltacatalunya.cat). In June, the city centre is the setting for the bike and skating festival, the **Festa de la Bici i els Patins**, which attracts more than

15,000 participants (www.bcn.cat/festadelabici).

Practice

Barcelona biking
(Baixada de Sant Miquel, 6; T 93 285 38 32; www.barcelonabiking.com);

Al Punt de Trobada
(Badajoz, 24; T 93 225 05 85); **Barcelona by Bicycle** (Esparteria, 3; T 93 268 21 05) **Barcelona Bike** (Pas de sota Muralla, 3; T 93 269 02 04).

Athletics

In July, the Lluís Companys Olympic Stadium will be hosting the **City of Barcelona International Athletics Meeting**; the **Barcelona Marathon** is in March (www.maratobarcelona.com), and attracts more than 12,000 participants. And Barcelona's oldest and most prestigious race, the **Jean Bouin**, is in November. (www.elmundodeportivo.es).

Barcelona also plays host to some of the world's most massively attended community races. In April, the city hosts the 31st **Cursa del Corte Inglés** (www.cursaelcorteingles.net), which set a Guinness World Record in 1994 that remains unbeaten today, with over 109,457 participants. In April, the city hosts the firefighters' race, the 11th **Cursa Bombers** (www.cursabombers.com) and, in September, as part of the city's main festival, the 28th **Cursa de la Mercè** (www.bcn.cat/cursamerce).

Practice

There are also many areas for jogging (Carretera de les Aigües, Montjuïc, Park Güell, Parc de la Ciutadella, the waterfront, Parc de l'Oreneta...). The city has four athletics stadiums:

Estadi Municipal Joan Serrahima (Camí del Polvorí, 5-7; T 93 423 80); **Estadi Municipal Can Dragó** (Roselló i Porcel, 7-11; T 93 276 04 80); **Complex Esportiu Municipal Mar Bella** (Av. Litoral, 86-96; T 93 221 06 76); **Estadi de la Universitat de Barcelona** (Av. Diagonal, 695-701; T 93 403 93 70).

Swimming

In addition to its magnificent beaches, the city also has a wide range of swimming pools: **Aiguajoc, Centre de Fitness** (Comte Borrell, 21-33; T 93 443 03 35); **Club Natació Atlètic Barceloneta** (Pl. Del Mar, s/n; T 93 221 00 10); **Club Natació Catalunya** (Ramiro de Maeztu, 27; T 93 213 43 44); **Club Natació Montjuïc** (Segura, s/n; T 93 331 82 88); **Poliesportiu Marítim - Centre Talassoteràpia** (Pg. Marítim, 33; T 93 224 04 40); **Piscines Bernat Picornell** (Av. de l'Estadi, 30-40; T 93 423 40 41); **Piscina Municipal Perill** (Perill, 16-22; T 93 459 44 30); **Dir Diagonal** (Ganduxer, 25-27; T 93 202 22 02).

Skating

In June, you can skate through the city's streets and see the halfpipe displays by world champions at the **Festa de la Bici i els Patins**. (www.bcn.cat/festadelabici). All year round, the seafront is the ideal place to skate in safety (www.patinar-bcn.org).

To hire or buy skates: Cooltra (Passeig Joan de Borbó, 80-84; T 93 221 40 70); Inercia (Wellington, 88; T 93 486 92 56). For **ice-skating**: Skating (Roger de Flor, 168; T 93 245 28 00).

FC Barcelona Stadium

Practical guide